WHERE HAVE ALL THE SENIOR WOMEN GONE?

WHERE HAVE ALL THE SENIOR WOMEN GONE?

Nine Critical Job Assignments for
Women Leaders

Ines Wichert

First published 2011 by
PALGRAVE MACMILLAN

Palgrave Macmillan in the UK is an imprint of Macmillan Publishers Limited, registered in England, company number 785998, of Houndmills, Basingstoke, Hampshire RG21 6XS.

Palgrave Macmillan in the US is a division of St Martin's Press LLC, 175 Fifth Avenue, New York, NY 10010.

Palgrave Macmillan is the global academic imprint of the above companies and has companies and representatives throughout the world.

Palgrave® and Macmillan® are registered trademarks in the United States, the United Kingdom, Europe and other countries.

ISBN 978–0–230–30129–0

This book is printed on paper suitable for recycling and made from fully managed and sustained forest sources. Logging, pulping and manufacturing processes are expected to conform to the environmental regulations of the country of origin.

A catalogue record for this book is available from the British Library.

A catalog record for this book is available from the Library of Congress.

10 9 8 7 6 5 4 3 2 1
20 19 18 17 16 15 14 13 12 11

Printed and bound in Great Britain by
CPI Antony Rowe, Chippenham and Eastbourne

To Maximilian and Konrad

CONTENTS

ACKNOWLEDGMENTS

I would like to thank the 53 senior women and men who very generously gave their time, despite their incredibly busy diaries, to help me explore the importance that critical job assignments have for women's careers. Every one of the interviewees had an inspirational story to tell and invaluable insights to share. I am very grateful for their frankness, their thoughtfulness and their desire to share their lessons learned with others. It was a great privilege to talk to every one of them.

I would also like to thank Tamsin Martin, Gaynor Davies and Mike Vessey for their comments on earlier drafts of this book, which were tremendously helpful; and thanks too to Eleanor Davey Corrigan for her editorial support.

Finally, and most importantly, I would like to thank my husband, Jason Rolles, for his unfailing encouragement. He has been the greatest supporter of this book.

INES WICHERT

CHAPTER OVERVIEW TABLE

Chapter	Job-specific challenges	Women-specific challenges
Introduction	• Purpose of this book • The structure of this book • How to use this book • The study	N/A
1 Where Are All the Senior Women?	• A gendered experience of work • A lack of experience as another barrier • Functional versus line roles • Learning on the job and building your CV • The study • Summary	N/A
2 In the Right Place at the Right Time	• High flyers, jugglers, authentic contributors – women's career phases • Timing critical job assignments across career phases • Career planning • Summary	N/A
3 Being Selected for Critical Job Assignments	• The importance of networks • Asking for promotion • The acceptability of self-promotion • Taking charge • Getting critical job assignments • Summary	N/A
4 The Early Stretch Assignment: Starting Off on the Fast Track	• Out of your depth • Working with senior managers • Building credibility • Learning about the organization and about yourself	• Building credibility in a male-dominated environment
5 International Assignments and Global Roles: Working Abroad	• Getting the role • Out there on your own • Being on the outside • My tried and tested approaches don't work here • Leading global virtual teams • Coming home	• Working in patriarchal societies • Transnational couples and trailing families

Lessons learned	Career benefits	In Focus
N/A	N/A	• N/A
N/A	N/A	• The Importance of Getting the Right Job Assignments
N/A	N/A	• The Critical Job Assignments Model
N/A	N/A	• Risk-Taking
• Self-confidence • Gaining a senior management perspective • Developing emotional intelligence	• Career acceleration through senior sponsorship • Building a reputation	• Sponsors
• Flexibility and adaptability • Resilience	• A big fish in a small pond • Understanding international business	• A Village of Support

Continued on next page

Chapter	Job-specific challenges	Women-specific challenges
6 Operational Experience: The Day-to-Day Running of a Business and P&L Accountability	• Being prepared for visible failure • The complexity of running a business	• Long hours, last-minute meetings and unplanned travel
7 People Management Responsibility: Building a High-Performance Team	• Building a strong direct team • Sorting out people problems • Engaging people • Delegating to gain headroom • Don't be afraid to assume authority	• Women as managers
8 Working in a Different Environment: New Roles, New Functions and New Industries	• A steep learning curve • A new culture and different expectations • Establishing credibility • Building new relationships	• A journey of self-discovery
9 Creating Something New: The Corporate Intrapreneur	• Devising a strategy and business plan • Building a support base • Establishing credibility • Dealing with resistance, bureaucracy and infrastructure constraints • Building the right team	• Serving the tea
10 Merging, Downsizing and Reengineering: The Change Agent	• The human element: dealing with emotions • Dealing with a lack of information and knowledge	• Dealing with male chauvinism and paternalistic thinking
11 Dealing with Problems and Crises: the Turnaround Pro	• Acting quickly and fixing problems • Re-establishing commitment • Working in a broken environment	• She shouldn't have this role
12 Joining The Executive Committee: Making It to the Top	• A big step up • Integrating with the executive team • Finding your voice (again)	• A vote of confidence
13 Conclusion: Where to Next?		• Career planning • Critical job assignments • Courage and curiosity • Connectedness

Lessons learned	Career benefits	In Focus
• Getting things done • Making decisions on your own	• Having credibility • Visibility	• Children and Career Advancement
• Making diversity work • Creating genuine engagement • Taking action sooner	• Creating a high-performance work environment • Delivering results time and again	• Role Models
• Using leadership skills rather than technical knowledge • Flexibility • Learning from others	• Becoming a well-rounded leader • Increased business acumen • Hitting the ground running	• Integrity and Cultural Fit
• If I can do this, I can do anything • Stakeholder management • Influencing others	• Demonstrating your capabilities and creating a legacy • Now I am visible	• Self-confidence
• Helping others to deal with change • Learning from senior stakeholders	• Being seen as a change agent • Seeing the organization more holistically • Innovation and vision	• Making Your Name
• Crisis management • Leading in times of crisis • Putting in place new processes	• Delivering results • Commitment and accountability	• Sensitivity
• I know what I'm talking about • Building senior management relationships • Working under pressure	• A wider influencing and decision-making remit • Delivering results at the most senior level	• Networking With Men
N/A	N/A	• A Reminder: Self-doubts and Setbacks

LIST OF INTERVIEWEES

Helen Andreas, Group Head of Retail & Distribution, Vodafone plc
Wendy Antaw, Head of Information Systems, Land Securities Group plc
Gillian Berkmen, Brand and Commercial Director, Mothercare UK
Ltd
Julia Bond, Non-executive Director, CLCH
Kate Bostock, Executive Director, General Merchandise, Marks and
Spencer plc. Mother
Helen Buck, Convenience Director, J Sainsbury plc. Mother
Jessica Burley, CEO, MCHI Ltd
Anna Capitanio, Vice-President Organizational Effectiveness and
M&A, BT Global Services. Mother
Emma Cariaga, Head of Strategic Projects, Land Securities Group plc.
Mother
Alison Carnwath, Chairman, Land Securities Group plc
Paola Cuneo, General Manager, BT Group plc. Mother
Karen Dolenec, Financial Managing Director, Terra Firma Capital
Partners Ltd. Mother
Monique Dumas, Investor Relations and Communications Partner,
Electra Partners LLP
Carolyn Fairbairn, Group Development and Strategy Director, ITV plc.
Mother
Ana Garcia Fau, CEO, Yell Publicidad S.A., Spain. Mother
Irene Garcia-Sacedon, Operations Development Manager, Tesco plc
Susan Henderson, Company Secretary, Smith & Nephew plc. Mother
Alison Horrocks, Senior Vice-President, Corporate Governance and
Company Secretary, Inmarsat Group plc. Mother
Orlagh Hunt, Group Human Resources Director, RSA Group plc.
Mother
Claire Jenkins, Group Director, Corporate Affairs, Rexam plc
Margaret Johnson, Group CEO, Leagas Delaney Ltd.
Charlotte Lambkin, Group Communications Director, BAE Systems plc

Sophie Turner Laing, Managing Director, Entertainment and News, British Sky Broadcasting Ltd. Mother

Amanda Mackenzie, Group Marketing Director, Aviva plc. Mother

Anja Madsen, Operations Development Manager, Tesco plc

Helen Mahy, Company Secretary & General Counsel, National Grid plc

Catherine May, Group Director of Corporate Affairs, Centrica plc. Mother

Anne Minto OBE, Group Director, Human Resources, Centrica plc

Jenny Newton, Senior Manager, Information Technology Industry. Mother

Karen Oddey, CEO of an equity-funded specialist electronics company

Pat O'Driscoll, Operational Managing Director, Terra Firma Capital Partners Ltd

Anne Mette Ovrum, Property Manager, Kongsvinger kommune, Norway. Mother

Jo Pisani, Partner, PricewaterhouseCoopers LLP. Mother

Cathryn Riley, UK Commercial Director, Aviva plc

Hana Rolles, Head of Online Marketing and Sales, Vodafone plc

Amelia Santos, Operations Development Manager, Tesco plc. Mother

Katherine Stone, Global Talent Manager, Unilever plc

Priscilla Vacassin, Group HR Director, Prudential plc. Mother

Lois Wark, Group Corporate Communications Manager, Randgold Resources plc. Mother

Sheelagh Whittaker, Non-executive Director, Standard Life plc. Mother

Expert opinion

Andy Doyle, Group HR Director, ITV plc
Elin Hurvenes, Founder, Professional Boards Forum UK and Norway
Mary Lawrance, Founder of Cariance, Executive Search
Bill Parsons, EVP, Human Resources, ARM Ltd.

Anonymous contributions

CEO, UK company. Mother
HR Director, FTSE 100 company. Mother
Senior manager, Fortune 500 company, USA. Mother

Senior manager, FTSE 100 company
Senior manager, Royal Bank of Scotland plc
Senior manager, finance industry. Mother
Senior manager, property industry. Mother
Senior manager, Norway. Mother
Senior manager, FTSE 100 company

The title given for each of the interviewees is that held at the time of the interview. A significant number of the interviewees also hold non-executive directorships which are not listed.

All named quotes used in this book were signed off by the relevant interviewee. The generic title of 'Senior manager, FTSE 100 company' is used in cases where the interviewees have asked for their contributions to remain anonymous. More descriptive titles, such as 'HR Director, FTSE 100 company' or 'Senior manager, finance industry' are only used where at least five interviewees fall into this category of description. Some quotes have been altered slightly to protect anonymity and confidentiality.

INTRODUCTION

The 1990s began to see an increasing readiness of organizations to promote women to senior management positions; however, not much progress has been made since then.[1] This is a disappointing state of affairs, given that it now often starts so well: girls are outperforming boys in education, with girls obtaining more GCSEs and doing better than their male peers in many subjects at A-level.[2,3] While young men and women are almost equally likely to obtain a first class degree, more young women than men are likely to achieve an upper second.[4] In many industries young women enter professional careers in similar numbers to their male counterparts and during the initial years make comparable progress. However, as both men and women start to progress further in their careers, take on more responsibility and reach their thirties, things start to go awry for many women in the corporate world. While there is still a good representation at middle management level, women's under-representation in decision-making jobs at the top of organizations is significant.[5] A report by the British Equal Opportunity Commission (EOC) highlights that, out of a total of over 31,000 top jobs, just under 10,000 are filled by women.[6] For example, only 124 out of 1,119 FTSE 100 directorships are held by women, and only 125 out of 646 Members of Parliament (MPs) are women. The Female FTSE 100 Board Index, which examines women's representation at senior management level across all FTSE 100 companies, shows that almost a quarter of the UK's leading organizations (21/100) still do not have a single woman at board level.[7] The picture looks even less encouraging when the Index turns to female executive directors. Only 16 FTSE 100 companies have female executive directors.

THE PURPOSE OF THE BOOK

Women's reduced career progression has been attributed to various cultural and structural barriers such as gender stereotyping, society's expectations of women, and childcare arrangements. Another area that is attracting increasing interest is women's career choices and the lack of certain types of experiences on their CV. Many business leaders call on women to get more operational experience and take on international assignments, but little dedicated attention has been paid to which types of experience really matter for women. Are operational experience and international assignments the most important types of assignments a woman needs on her CV? If so, how do they help her career progression, and what are the challenges women typically face during these assignments? Are there other experiences or roles that are important for women's career progression, and is there an ideal time for any such assignments during a woman's career? This book tries to answer some of these questions and draws attention to the critical job assignments that successful women have found to be essential in developing their leadership skills and, equally important, in building a credible CV. It does, however, not intend to provide a precise road map or blueprint for progressing to the top; every career progresses along a different path.

This book is inspired by many discussions I have had over the years with women at junior and middle management level who are lost as to what to do next. Many have developed great technical expertise and have moved on to their first or second management role, but are unsure about their next move. Even if a woman does not aspire to progress all the way to a senior executive role, this book will still provide important insights into how to advance to more challenging assignments and how to build a fulfilling career. Many of the critical job assignments explored in this book, the challenges faced, the lessons learned and the career benefits gained apply equally to men. However, this book explores all these aspects through the eyes of some of the most senior women in UK and international business, and the analysis provides a unique female angle on the topic of critical job assignments. The female voice provides inspiration for women but also vital learning and insights for male senior managers, human resource (HR) professionals and anyone else interested in the topic of women's career progression. The insights shared by the interviewees hold valid lessons for a wide audience, irrespective of its gender or background.

THE STRUCTURE OF THE BOOK

This book is split broadly into three parts. The first three chapters make up the introductory part. Chapter 1 sets out the current situation of women in senior management positions and introduces the idea of critical job assignments in more detail. Chapter 2 looks at women's career phases and the importance of timing critical job assignments. It also introduces the Critical Job Assignments Model. Finally, Chapter 3 explores selection and recruitment dynamics, and the importance of women being proactive when looking for critical job assignments. Part 2 explores nine different critical job assignments and looks in detail at the job- and women-specific challenges that the interviewees faced, the lessons they learnt and the career benefits they gained. Each chapter also explores the types of support the interviewees found beneficial and takes a look at the timing of the assignment. The chapters finish with a short summary and with a list of suggested actions for those who want to take action on what they have just read in their own careers, or the careers of those who they support as managers, mentors, sponsors or HR professionals. The final part of this book provides a summary of the main learning and insights from the nine different job assignments.

HOW TO USE THE BOOK

This book is designed to provide both a comprehensive examination of the role of critical job assignments for a woman's career as well as a practical reference guide for job assignment obstacles that you may be encountering in your career right now. If one of the nine critical job assignments is of particular interest to you at the moment, you can turn to the relevant chapter straight away. Each chapter sets out the challenges you are likely to face, as well as the learning and the career benefits that you may take away. Furthermore, it provides suggestions for actions you may want to take. If, on the other hand, you are interested in learning more about the importance of career planning, mastering the make-or-break years or about finding out more effective career management strategies, Chapters 1 to 3 provide a useful overview of these topics. Throughout the book you will find In Focus sections which provide valuable insights and food for thought on career progression topics that have emerged as important alongside the critical job assignments. They will help you get a better understanding of some of the factors that interact with the nine critical job assignments and that may help or hinder your career progression as you consider your next career move.

THE STUDY

The content of this book is based on 53 interviews with senior women in mostly FTSE100 organizations and their international equivalents. The majority of the women hold either senior roles with direct access to the executive committee or are members of the executive committee. The sample also contains a small number of middle management career women and a number of experts, both male and female, in the areas of HR, executive search and leadership development. More information about the study is provided in Chapter 1 and in Appendix 1.

PART I

1

WHERE ARE ALL THE SENIOR WOMEN?

If you believe in yourself you can do it. But you need to work hard no matter how talented you are. You need to be committed and you will have to give up on some things and make sacrifices.

(Kate Bostock, Executive Director,
General Merchandise, Marks & Spencer)

Pursue your goal, go after whatever you want to do and don't be held back by the fact that you are a woman. It is immaterial that you are a woman.

(Lois Wark, Group Corporate Communications Manager,
Randgold Resources)

The call for more women to be represented at senior management level has changed from an argument about equality and fairness to one about business benefits. The business case for women at the top is strong and growing; almost half of the workforce and talent pool is female, and there is evidence that organizations with three or more women at board level do financially better when measured in the form of return on sales, return on equity and return on invested capital.[1] Nevertheless, there are still only very few women in senior leadership positions. There is no doubt that it takes tremendous commitment to make it to the top, and this applies to both men and women. Senior managers need to be determined and invest considerable amounts of time and energy in their jobs, and some argue that women have to be even more ambitious than men to make it to the top as they face additional hurdles along the way. Some of the reasons why women have a hard time getting to the top are increasingly well documented, and cultural and structural disadvantages are frequently held up as reasons for women's reduced career progression.

3

A GENDERED EXPERIENCE OF WORK

Cultural factors refer to beliefs and norms that women themselves (and society at large) hold about things such as what it means to be a woman, what women need and want, and what it means to be a leader. The impacts of these beliefs and norms are felt in many different ways. For example, while it is regarded as 'natural' for men to progress to senior management roles, women are still expected to be the primary carers for children. Also, perceptions of leadership overlap to a large degree with beliefs of what it means to be a man. Decisiveness, risk-taking and competence are considered to be both male character traits and the qualities of a good leader. Leadership is far less readily associated with female traits, such as consensus-building, being communal and nurturing.[2] Stereotypes of women and their 'natural' characteristics are often so deep-seated that women who act against these expectations are often seen in a negative light. Women who are perceived to be assertive or self-promoting – both traits that tend to be regarded positively in men – are often marginalized at work and receive unfavourable feedback about their leadership style.[3]

Structural factors refer to the processes and structures that women encounter in their lives. These include, for example, promotion processes at work and the division of labour at home. Most big corporations expect their employees to follow a traditional, linear path of career advancement. While most men are able to meet these expectations, women's need for periods of time out and flexible work arrangements in order to raise children does not always allow them to remain on a linear career trajectory as easily as men.[4] At this stage, women frequently opt out of their fast track careers into second-tier roles, or remain in practitioner roles that give them more flexibility.[5] Such flexible work arrangements are often stigmatized in organizations, however, and as a result, women's commitment to the organizational course is questioned. Another example of a structural barrier that women encounter in the workplace is the age restriction that can be associated with talent pools. Only if employees have reached a certain position in the organization by a certain age are they deemed to have the necessary talent and drive to be considered as possible contenders for senior management roles. Women who take time out for maternity leave and who work part-time for a number of years often exceed the upper age restriction of the talent pools before they have reached a senior enough role and therefore miss out on further career opportunities.[6] Other barriers frequently mentioned are the exclusion of women from informal networks, the lack of mentoring, a shortage of role models, the lack of accountability on the part of senior leaders, and limited opportunities for visibility.[7]

A number of these barriers can be very subtle and may in many cases even be unintentional on the part of the organization. Meyerson states that while in the past discrimination was overt and could be tackled through strong rhetoric and legal action, today's discrimination has largely gone underground. She calls it a 'problem without a name'.[8] And this problem without a name is encountered by women at every turn of their careers. Eagly and Carli examined a series of studies on wage and promotion prospects for men and women, and concluded that wage and promotion discrimination does not seem to get stronger as women get to the top of organizations – it is equally strong at every stage of a woman's career. The authors therefore conclude that the metaphor of the glass ceiling is not appropriate and instead propose the metaphor of a *labyrinth*, where women get lost and disappear on the way to the top rather than at the penultimate stage.[9]

A LACK OF EXPERIENCE AS ANOTHER BARRIER

While these cultural and structural factors clearly play a significant role in women's reduced progression to the top roles, other important but much less well understood factors are women's career histories and work experience. While not every career will progress along the same path and not every senior manager will have gone through the same experiences, there seem to be some common formative experiences and roles that help aspiring women to prove themselves in a business setting and to acquire the foundation from which to progress to a senior management role. Chief executive officers (CEOs) repeatedly mention women's lack of experience as a reason why they do not make it to senior levels.[10]

Profit and loss (P&L) accountability, the experience of the day-to-day running of an organization's operation, and exposure to senior management decision-making are often mentioned as core prerequisites for senior managers.[11,12]

When recruiting for a new group marketing director, the HR director of a large FTSE 100 company set out what the senior management was looking for:

> We are looking for core leadership skills including intellectual capability to deal with complex business issues, operations experience,

communication skills, working in a matrix organization, a persuasive style, working with others, and drive. You need to be able to run large teams … Running organizational change would also be important for a group marketing director.

And in general:

Running a business is not important for a human resources director but it is for commercial roles. Also, working in different functions and industry sectors shows adaptability which is an important characteristic. Generally, you need broad-based skills for senior management roles. You need operational capability and you need to have run something of scale, for example, a team, operations, sales. You need to be able to demonstrate that you can either operate at scale or that you have a very broad background. (HR director, FTSE 100 company)

The human resources director of another FTSE 100 company recalls the recent recruitment process for a chief information officer (CIO) role:

Out of 50 applications there was not a single woman who applied. You need a first or 2.1 from a top university … Ideally, people should have an MBA. Experience we were looking for in the CIO candidates: running big IT projects and running different departments. We need someone who has had a spectacular career to date and someone who is looking to be the top person for the first time. Most people were Number Twos looking for their first Number One job. The candidate we chose in the end had not gone straight into IT but had experience of different functions. He had experience of strategic planning and supply chain. He had first worked at three to four different divisions at a former employer and then held four or five progressively more senior IT roles. My organisation is looking for well-rounded people. Innovation is improved by boundary spanning: different cultures, different countries, different companies … it demonstrates evidence that people have adapted. (HR director, FTSE 100 company)

Here is what the MD of an executive search firm had to say about what makes a good CV:

The numbers … They are evidence of results, for example, sales numbers and P&L. Also things such as opening an operation in a new country, taking on something tough and turning it around, or line responsibility. [Recruiters] will look at the sorts of teams you are leading and whether you are growing or developing something interesting. Have you done something special? You also need industry knowledge and business acumen. International experience is not always essential. You don't have to move but you need to be able to travel. And, of course, sheer resilience. Sometimes roles are very nasty and high profile, so you need mental toughness. You need to be able to take the slings and arrows. Women don't lack that but men are better at showing it at interview. Recruiters ask themselves whether a woman will be able to stand up because it will be harder for her. (Mary Lawrance, Owner of Cariance, Executive Search)

Clearly, breadth of roles, dealing with increasing levels of scope and complexity, operational experience, working with and leading others, and resilience are top of the list when senior decision-makers consider the credentials of applicants. Women's career choices may, however, not always allow them to obtain the types of experience that senior decision-makers are looking for, as we shall see in the next section.

FUNCTIONAL VERSUS LINE ROLES

Women tend to be in functional roles,[13] such as human resources, IT, marketing, legal or finance, and much less frequently in line roles with P&L accountability and responsibility for the day-to-day running of the organization. Women often choose career paths that do not allow them to move to the top as their career choices do not position them at the centre of organizations but rather in peripheral support functions, which are not regarded as instrumental to the success of the organization in the eyes of senior managers. As a result, their business acumen is questioned. Choosing roles that are key to the organization's success is therefore an important element of a successful career as it will allow women to obtain visibility, business credibility and organizational power.[14] Cox and Cooper found that the managing directors in their study had gained exposure to many different types of challenges and parts of the organization by spending two to three years in a role before moving on. Moving to different companies, including smaller companies which provided exposure to much broader business issues than is often possible in a large organization, was another important element of their career progression.[15] These smaller incubator organizations give women the opportunity to learn about many different functions.[16] There is evidence that moving frequently between business-critical functions early on in one's working life puts in place crucial foundations for a successful career. However, there is also evidence that women tend to enter and stay in support functions, often becoming specialists and thus reducing their ability to build broad-based foundations for their career. Managers who progress within the same function are more likely to derail than managers who have faced a series of different challenges in different parts of an organization. Their broad experience base allows them to build up detailed knowledge of how their organization works.[17] We shall see in Chapter 6 why women may choose functional over operational roles.

LEARNING ON THE JOB AND BUILDING A CV

The requirements for senior management roles, and particularly so the top role of the CEO, are demanding. Not only does it take commitment, intelligence and leadership qualities to get to the top, as we saw earlier, it also requires the right set of experiences to be deemed eligible for roles in the upper echelons of an organization. Leadership development experts agree that the best way to cultivate talented employees for the top jobs is in the form of stretching assignments and new roles along the way.[18] When it comes to honing the abilities and experiences that leaders need in order to succeed, on-the-job experience is hard to beat. McCall and colleagues introduced the 70–20–10 rule in the late 1980s, which is still referred to regularly now. It states that 70 per cent of all leadership development results from on-the-job learning, with only 20 per cent coming from coaching and 10 per cent from formal training.[19] On-the-job learning, particularly when it provides a move away from a person's comfort zone, increases adaptivity, resourcefulness and resilience.[20] On-the-job learning is at its best when it stretches a person; neither too easy nor overwhelming assignments will provide the desired learning.[21] John Adair states that 'stretching is painful but it is the only way to gain stature' (p. 115).[22] Dotlich and colleagues compare a stretch assignment to the slaying of the beast or completing the odyssey in the mythical world. Stretch assignments are defined as those projects for which a person does not have the necessary skills, expertise and experience.[23]

8

IN FOCUS: THE IMPORTANCE OF GETTING THE RIGHT JOB ASSIGNMENTS

The right job assignments quite simply allow someone to show what they can do. They bring out a person's full potential, stretch them and help them to take a big leap forward on the career ladder by helping to build a strong personal reputation. In the words of a human resources director at a large financial institution: 'Job roles are hugely important. Great roles propel people onwards. Look for roles that allow you to shine and roles that allow you to make good contacts' (Orlagh Hunt, Group Human Resources Director, RSA Group).

However, getting the right assignment is not in and of itself a guarantee of success; it depends on what a woman makes of it. Full commitment to delivering in a role is a prerequisite to using a role to make your mark:

Job roles are important but you can change your role. If you see potential for growth in the role or if you see that there is more you can add, do it. It is about what you make of your role. (Senior manager, FTSE 100 company)

While there is a clear element of making the most of the role you are in and shaping it to the best of your talents, there seems to be a 'perfect' role that comes along once or twice during a woman's career. We shall see more in Chapter 10 about these 'making your name' roles.

The interview data from the study that underpins the findings in this book tell us more about the critical job experiences of almost 50 of the most senior businesswomen in FTSE 100 companies and their international equivalents. Many of the interviewees benefited from being offered new job assignments that gave them the opportunity to prove themselves and to further develop their track record. Equally, though, they talked about being offered roles that were not exactly what they were looking for. But they still felt that the opportunity was worth taking as it either gave them an entry point to a new organization or a new industry sector. In these cases, the interviewees were very clear that while they were happy to take on the role, they only wanted to do it for a limited amount of time and then move on to a new and challenging activity. After delivering in the roles they were brought in to tackle – in their typical manner of outstanding delivery – the organizations generally kept their promises and provided the women with the jobs they were looking for. As the women had by then proved themselves in the new organization, senior managers were often comfortable to take a risk and give the women the opportunity to work in a field that was new to them. A number of the interviewees also talked about the importance of knowing when to stick it out in a difficult role and when to move on:

> I moved from an operational role into a conceptual role. It took me longer than usual to settle into the role. There were different ways of measuring success. I moved from an output-focused success model in my operational roles to now being rewarded for my inputs and thinking. I felt that the role was not right for me but my boss convinced me to give it another go. I stuck it out and did the role for a few more years. Once I had overcome the initial problems with the new way of working the role turned out to be pivotal for me. It gave me confidence that I can deliver just as successfully as a conceptual thinker than [I can] as an operational deliverer. The experience from this role formed one of the pillars for a move to a senior role later on, where I took a company through a time of real adversity. (Senior manager, FTSE 100 company)

Various leadership writers and scholars have explored the types of on-the-job development opportunities that provide the learning future senior leaders need. Each of them uses slightly different terminology and a somewhat different focus: McCall and colleagues talk about lessons of experience, Dotlich and colleagues about leadership passages, McCauley about developmental job components, and Madsen about positions and assignments.[24,25,26,27] Nevertheless, there seems to be broad agreement about the types of on-the-job development opportunities that each has found to be important for a leader's development. The list of these potential development opportunities is long and varied.

Getting to grips with an *early challenge* is an important starting point for many senior women and men. Being thrown in at the deep end and learning to cope with difficult situations provides women with a belief in themselves as well as the opportunity to prove to others what they can do. *Changing jobs, moving from line to functional roles* and vice versa, and moving to *new institutions* allows talented managers to learn to deal with unfamiliar responsibility, new challenges and complexity. It broadens their leadership skills, helps them to develop new networks, and generally provides the steep learning curve associated with being in a new environment. *Starting something new* allows a manager to learn to set new directions and also provides opportunities to demonstrate the ability to grow a business venture from nothing into something substantial, which is another beneficial experience reported by senior women. *Becoming a member of a task force or joining a committee* helps managers to learn to work across the organization and to gain in-depth knowledge about how the organization works. It also puts them into contact with new and different stakeholders, and helps them to learn how to influence without positional power. *Managing people* teaches aspiring leaders how to deal with people problems, underperformance and how to harness the power of diverse teams. *Working abroad* teaches managers to deal with diversity across cultures, while *turnaround jobs* allow a person to learn to deal with inherited problems. Other roles that are seen to be developmental are those of *running a business* and *being part of a merger or an acquisition*.

There is clearly some overlap between senior managers' wish lists for desirable work experience and the development opportunities listed above, but together they make for a long list of 'tick boxes'. The research presented in this book attempts to address this problem and sets out the top nine critical job assignments that combine important personal development *and* CV building. Critical job assignments in this book are defined mainly as job roles but also as special, one-off projects as part of a role, secondments, a task force or committee work.

THE STUDY

The book is based on two main sources of information: first, in-depth interviews with 53 female senior managers of FTSE 100 companies and their international equivalents, and with subject matter experts in the area of women and leadership; and, second, existing academic research. The content and structure of the book are determined by the interview findings, with the research literature being used to further elaborate and explore some of the key themes that emerged during the interviews.

Of the 53 interviews, 49 were conducted with senior women in FTSE 100 companies or their international equivalents. The remaining four interviews were conducted with male and female subject matter experts in the area of leadership development and career progression. The senior women's average age was 45 and their average work experience 22 years. The majority of the senior women were married (65 percent) with another 22 percent living with a partner.

57 percent (28 of the 49) women have children, with 39 percent of the interviewees stating that childcare responsibilities were shared fully with their spouses. The average age at which the interviewees had their first child was 32 years. The interviewees represent many different industry sectors, with finance, retail, telecoms and energy being those most strongly represented. The interviewees had a high level of education, with only 8 percent stating that they did not have a first degree. Almost half of the interviewees had an undergraduate degree (49 percent) as their highest level of education, while around another quarter (27 percent) have an MBA, and 16 per cent another type of postgraduate qualification as their highest level of qualification. Not surprisingly, the majority of the interviewees have a functional background, with human resources, strategy, communications and legal being most strongly represented. Only 14 of the 49 interviewees (28 percent) had a general management background. 17 of the 53 interviewees (30 percent) were of nationalities other than British. These interviewees come from northern Europe (Sweden, Denmark and Norway), southern Europe (for example, Italy and Spain), Australia, North America and South Africa. Appendix 1 provides more background information about the study's methodology, the interview sample and the data analysis.

During the interviews I asked the senior women about their most critical job assignments to date; critical from a developmental as well as from a credibility building point of view. What were the 'game-changers'? In most interviews I explored two different critical job assignments in depth, and in total 112 job assignments were explored. The following nine critical job assignments were identified by the interviewees as the most important career milestones:

- The early stretch assignment: starting off on the fast track.
- International assignments and global roles: working abroad.
- Operational experience: the day-to-day running of a business and P&L accountability.
- People management responsibility: building a high-performance team.

- Working in a different environment: new roles, new functions and new industries.
- Creating something new: the corporate intrapreneur.
- Merging, downsizing and reengineering: the change agent.
- Dealing with problems and crises: the turnaround pro.
- Joining the executive committee: making it to the top.

Before each of the nine job assignments are looked at in more detail (starting from Chapter 4), we need to explore the importance of timing and strategic career planning across women's career phases. This is done in the next chapter, and provides an important backdrop to the chapters that follow.

SUMMARY

Women are still underrepresented at the top of many organizations. Cultural and structural barriers, such as beliefs about what it means to be a woman, desirable attributes for leaders and childcare arrangements are often cited as the reasons for why women do not make it to the top as readily as men. Another reason for women's reduced progression to senior roles may be their lack of certain types of experience such as P&L accountability and the day-to-day running of an organization's operations. Senior decision-makers value this experience as it provides evidence of having a broad base and having worked to scale and in complex situations. Women's predominant focus on functional roles may, however, mean that they do not get enough exposure to the types of experience that senior leaders want. In addition to what senior leaders deem to be essential foundations for a move to top roles, leadership scholars draw attention to experiences that allow aspiring leaders to hone their skills, such as early stretch assignments, moving between functional and operational roles, people management, and a host of other business challenges. The study that underpins the work presented in this book identifies the nine most important critical job assignments that have allowed senior female FTSE 100 leaders both to develop personally and to build a credible CV.

2

IN THE RIGHT PLACE AT THE RIGHT TIME

Timing doesn't always work out the way you expect it. Don't be too narrow in your planning.
(Karen Dolenec, Financial Managing Director,
Terra Firma Capital Partners)

You need to know who the three most important people for your career are in your organization. Who has the most influence over your career progress? You need to feed back to them regularly and keep them informed, and you need to be vocal about what you want to do.
(Elin Hurvenes, Founder of the Professional Boards Forum,
Norway and UK)

Women's work participation and education levels are becoming increasingly similar to those of men across the developed world, and careers have also become increasingly important for women in recent decades. Delaying child-bearing, returning to work after maternity leave, and in some (admittedly rare) cases even consciously deciding not to have children, are signs that women are serious about their careers. Until relatively recently, however, careers were the domain of men and as such they are still defined with reference to men and their typical progression paths. Even today, a career is more often than not defined as 'an ordered sequence of development extending over a period of years and the introduction of progressively more responsible roles within an occupation' (p. 184).[1] This definition is often referred to as a *stage theory* of career progression and is based on the assumption of a linear and predictable progression of positions with increasing levels of accountability and compensation.[2] It is widely used and drives organizations' expectations and actions about their employees' careers. Unfortunately for many women, though, it is a definition that typically bears little resemblance to their work realities. While women tend to progress as fast as men in the early years of their careers, sharing similar experiences and aspirations, soon experiences start to diverge.[3] When a woman reaches her late twenties or her thirties, she has to make some difficult decisions about whether to focus on her career or to start a family. Mason and Mason Ekman point out that a woman's thirties are often her toughest time, and if she chooses to have a family her career prospects start to change dramatically. The odds of her making it to the top are beginning to stack up against her, and it is not only a problem of women trailing men in their career progression as a result of the time taken out for maternity leave.[4] Once childcare responsibilities are present, women tend to shoulder the majority of this responsibility at home even when they return to full-time work. Hochschild calls this additional responsibility the 'second shift'.[5] It causes a double burden – of dealing with childcare and household responsibilities in addition to a demanding job – and is exhausting for women. Even those women who can afford household help still have to deal with arranging this help and organizing chores in the background. At work, women's need for flexibility to accommodate these additional duties is taken as a sign of decreased commitment to the organization and acts as a continual brake on career progression. Once women have children, in the minds of their managers and co-workers they leave the high-potential track and are put on a 'mommy track': 'She will not want to do this project as she cannot travel with children', 'She couldn't attend tonight's emergency meeting because of childcare constraints; she is not fully committed to the project' and so on. As a result of this dual load of maintaining a demanding career and bringing up a young family, many women often abandon the fast track to enable them to accommodate their roles as mothers; however, fathers rarely do the same. As Mason and Mason Ekman point out: 'men and women are no longer on equal footing' (p. 24).[6] Men's and women's lives diverge dramatically – both at work and outside it.

An increasing number of women try to progress their careers and return to work full-time.[7] Almost without exception this means having to turn into 'superwoman' to deal with the demands of both work and home, and living with the guilt of not doing justice to either the home or the work role. Time out or a step back are not uncommon consequences of 'burning out' after trying to combine an executive career with having a young family. However, after a short period of time out women return with new energy. As their children get older and a number of career disappointments, such as blocked promotions and discrimination, have been dealt with, women tend to report a return to calmer career waters. Let us take a closer look at the various career phases women pass through on their way to the top, and examine their respective challenges in more detail.

HIGH FLYERS, JUGGLERS, AUTHENTIC CONTRIBUTORS: WOMEN'S CAREER PHASES

Numerous studies have looked at successful women and have tried to chart women's career phases.[8,9,10] There seem to be three broad phases, which I have called High Flyers, Jugglers and Authentic Contributors.

High flyers – working hard and going places

The first career phase, which tends to run from a woman's mid-twenties to her early thirties, is characterized by women being proactive in progressing their careers and by feeling in charge of this progress, a concept that is often referred to as an internal career locus of control. Women feel they can realize their ambitions of organizational success and are determined to rise above barriers to advancement. 'Do and have it all' is a leading mantra for this age group.[11] This is a time of intense learning and development at work, and the point at which a woman establishes herself as a high achiever.[12] Demonstrating the stamina for hard work and long hours, showing the ability to get to grips with difficult assignments, being able to find a good mentor and learning to network effectively are important lessons learned during this phase.[13] Women's career experiences during this first phase are not much different than those of their male counterparts, and it could be argued that in many respects this first phase is gender neutral. However, toward the end of this phase the women in this group, many of whom are still childless, are increasingly thinking about how to combine their career ambitions with their desire to start a family.[14]

Progressing faster than men

During this first phase of a woman's career something else seems to be happening – women actually progress faster than their male colleagues. There is evidence that, compared to men, women tend to

16

be significantly younger when they make it to the top, they are less likely to have been with the organization all their lives, and they have spent less time on average in each job. As a result, if women make it to the top, they apparently get there faster. Some surveys show an age difference between women and men of eight years at any management level. Counter to general perception, younger women (under the age of 35) also occupy more general management and strategic roles than their male counterparts.[15,16,17] Powell and Butterfield suggest that appointment panels give preference to applicants with fewer years of work experience.[18] Panels were found to be impressed by high flyers who could demonstrate accomplishments and performance within a limited time-frame. This may be a sign that the glass ceiling is permeable for those women who progress at a fast rate early in their careers.[19] However, this advantage diminishes as women get older, and as the average age of reaching senior positions decreases, delays in promotions are bound to become more damaging to a woman's chances of getting to the top. Three possible explanations have been offered to explain this phenomenon of women progressing more quickly early on.[20] First, younger women have been raised with the expectation of equal opportunities and have in many cases received equal challenges and development opportunities early in life. These information-age 'Generation X' women, with little loyalty to companies, see themselves as being in charge of their own destinies and take advantage of career opportunities as they emerge. The second explanation focuses on women's age. Young women may be seen as 'a-gendered high flyers' in their first career phase and may therefore be put on an equal footing with male counterparts. Women only start to be perceived as female when they start a family, often in their thirties. Therefore the glass ceiling is still in place and continues to hold back older women while allowing younger women through. The third explanation offered is that the glass ceiling has moved upward. As women work hard, are tenacious and extremely good at what they do, they overcome barriers much more easily than their predecessors. However, the 'old boys' club' still operates at the upper end of senior management, making it difficult for women to progress to the very top of an organization.

A note of caution. Fast progression must not turn into a ticking off of roles and a race to the next level without taking on board the lessons from the current role. There is substantial evidence that where women have not learned from setbacks along the way they may lack both resilience and the necessary networks to deal with obstacles later.[21,22,23]

And setbacks *will* come, as no career progresses without them. They may take different forms: a failed project, being passed over for promotion, being made redundant, falling out with senior management, for example. Furthermore, it is important to understand that not every stretch assignment can lead to a job promotion. Numerous interviewees talked about first building a broad base, involving a number of lateral moves, before starting on an upward trajectory. As has already been mentioned in Chapter 1, some of the interviewees also talked about agreeing to take on a role similar to one they had previously held, but for a new employer, on the understanding that once she had helped the organization to deal with its problems, the organization would provide the woman with the role she really wanted.

During this first phase women need stretching assignments that allow them to learn skills and find their strengths. Coaching and mentoring to help increase confidence levels during this phase are also important.[24,25]

Jugglers: the make-or-break years

The second broad phase covers a woman's early thirties to mid-forties. During their thirties women have to take notice of their biological clock and decide whether to have children or not.[26] It has been argued that the turmoil of these middle years is because of the many choices women have to make during this time with regard to starting a family and fully committing to their careers. The juggling of career and motherhood is a central theme at this time.[27]

The make-or-break years

The most testing time during a woman's career is undoubtedly when she starts a family and takes on caring responsibilities for young children, particularly so when this also coincides with the period when the foundations for the move to the top are being laid, usually in a woman's thirties.[28,29] After acquiring technical competence and first management experience during her twenties, the thirties bring more management responsibility and higher-visibility projects, which are often associated with long hours, travel and a full commitment to the organization. Management consultancy McKinsey looked at what experiences shape careers in a survey of almost 900 male and female executives from around the world.[30] When asked about timing, respondents indicated that their most important career-shaping event happened around the age of 30, after they had been in work for about eight years, usually in the form of a new role. It is during this time that employees with talent and commitment are noticed and earmarked for greater things. It is, however, also often around this time that women decide to begin a family and, as a result, need more flexibility, take time out and often take a step back in their career. Working full-time and giving maximum commitment to the organization to tackle the difficult middle-to-senior-management hurdle rarely combines well with raising a young family, as the comment below illustrates well:

> Moving from middle to senior management means that you have to take on additional responsibilities ... It also means additional time sacrifice. Sometimes it's a choice and some women may not want to do that. You need to create additional outputs and shoulder [additional] responsibility. (Lois Wark, Group Corporate Communications Manager, Randgold Resources)

Mason and Mason Ekman call a woman's thirties her 'make-or-break' years. Mothers who make it past the make-or-break years successfully continue to flourish in their careers later. However, only 40–60 percent of the women who make it past this time have children. The main winners in the make-or-break years are men with children. Men on a steep career path are more likely to have children than women who have dedicated themselves to their career.[31]

Ordering career and motherhood

Ordering career and motherhood is an important career strategy that might help women advance to senior positions.[32] Unless the main parenting responsibility is taken on by the woman's partner, women have to give priority to parenting over career and vice versa at various points in their lives.[33] Two different routes are usually talked about: either having children early before the demands of a senior career kick in, or delaying child-bearing until the woman has reached a relatively senior position. A number of studies have shown that executive mothers feel that delaying having children is the better option for them, as working in a more senior role gives them more flexibility and allows them to observe how others manage work–life balance issues.[34] The senior interviewees in the study underpinning this book talked about having gained some breathing space and some level of organizational goodwill once they had moved to senior management positions. They were now drawing on this in order to deal with the extra demands of a young family. Increasingly, mothers with university degrees delay child-bearing until they are in their thirties.[35] Information from the Office for National Statistics in the UK shows that the number of women who give birth in their forties doubled between 1995 and 2005 (from 11,000 to 22,000). And more women than ever before are having children in their thirties (from 6 percent to 11 percent since the 1970s).[36] A study of female partners in a law firm showed that 60 percent of female partners had no children, and those who had children had often deferred child-bearing until after achieving partnership status.[37] And a study of women in middle management in IT found that almost a third had put off child-bearing to advance their careers. Women are, however, rarely rewarded for this commitment to their work, and men are almost three times as likely as women to advance to executive-level positions.[38] Once women have children in their thirties or early forties, many of them take minimum career beaks, as they fear stepping off the fast track.[39] But in an attempt to balance job and home responsibilities, women may drop to what Mason and Mason Ekman call the 'second tier'. Once on this second tier, reentry to the prestigious fast track is, however, very difficult, as reduced hours or part-time roles are not valued by organizations, and women lose their high-potential attributes in the eyes of those around them. As large organizations do not tend to pursue the ruthless 'up or out' rule of many consultancy or law firms, women do not drop out completely, but tend to get stuck at the bottom of the management hierarchy.[40]

Women who had put their families first and had children at a younger age talked about the benefits of being able to dedicate time to family demands while not having to deal with the demands of senior roles. These women accepted a slower route to the top while raising their children. Time away from work and part-time working were part of these women's paths to the top. Once their children were older, they accelerated their career advancement by concentrating fully on their career.[41,42] The interviewees in this book who had their children early and started their careers later talked about being proactive in seeking opportunities, asking for more responsibility and being courageous in taking on new challenges in order to catch up with their contemporaries on the career ladder.

Not all women order motherhood and career and instead try to combine them both. These women have career histories that resemble male, linear career progression, and in many cases they are the main breadwinner. These women rely on intensive outsourcing to make it all happen, which involves passing the main parenting responsibility either to their partner or another significant family member, who stays at home either temporarily or permanently to look after the children. These women rely on a complex set of relationships with others, both at work (mentors, work networks, supportive managers) and outside it (partners, parents, nannies, babysitters, cooks, household helps). Ezzedeen and Ritchy talk about a 'village of support'.[43]

Irrespective of how they have chosen to order motherhood and career (or not, for that matter), for many women in this second phase, the initial idealism has given way to pragmatism and doing what is necessary to get things done.[44] Women's career paths are more likely to be a mixture of both planned and unplanned moves. It is possible that at this mid-point women realize that the price for having it all, as desired in the early career phase, is too high, and they search for new career routes. During this time women's working lives are also strongly influenced by the relationships around them, both at work and outside it, and women increasingly have an external career locus of control as they recognize that nobody can progress without help from others. Many women around this time seem to hit a crisis point and report dissatisfaction, stalled careers, experiences of bad management and discrimination. They also start to move to different organizations in response to first encounters with the glass ceiling.[45,46]

Authentic contributors: a return to calmer waters

The third career phase, which spans the years from about 45 to around 60, sees a return to calmer waters, when career moves become more planned once again. In the early years of this final phase, women begin to come to terms with the challenges they faced during their often tumultuous thirties and early forties. While the demands of a younger family might not be completely over, increasing confidence is starting to allow a woman to find better ways of coping, and juggling turns into balancing out. This phase brings greater stability and allows women to consolidate and build further on previous achievements. While mentoring, good management and challenging assignments continue to be vital for women during this third career phase, organizational support, such as flexible work arrangements that allow a woman to achieve a work–life balance, are also crucial.[47]

Women focus on their career with renewed energy, but this new focus has a different nature. Whereas the early years were focused on personal satisfaction and success, the later years seem to be characterized more strongly by gaining satisfaction through contributing to the organization and to others, while at the same time maintaining a strong sense of self. Values have switched from achievement, competition and advancement to leading balanced lives that are enriched with recognition and respect. The external locus of control persists into this phase and women benefit most from being allowed to contribute the richness of their experience by mentoring and coaching others, and by generally passing on their knowledge and insights.

TIMING CRITICAL JOB ASSIGNMENTS ACROSS CAREER PHASES

Let us return to critical job assignments and examine whether there is a particularly good time for any one of them, given the various challenges and priorities across the three broad phases of women's careers. Which experiences can be acquired early in a career without taking away from the weight of the experience? Which job assignments are easiest to master while caring for young children? And to which job assignments does it become increasingly difficult to gain access the more senior a woman gets? It is unlikely that there is a blueprint or a one-size-fits-all solution for a successful career. Each of the 49 career histories examined is unique. However, across these career histories, a sequence of career steps has emerged. The Critical Job Assignments Model shown in Figure 2.1 provides an overview of these steps and the individual elements the interviewees identified as accelerators throughout their careers.

The ideal career begins with a degree in a numerate subject, which makes working with financial information second nature throughout a woman's career, and gives a head-start when it come to building credibility. This would be followed fairly quickly by an early stretch assignment at work, during which the woman demonstrates to herself and others what she is capable of doing. Increased visibility, sponsorship through senior management and personal confidence are important outcomes from this assignment. While still mobile and without children, broader and grittier roles follow which require flexibility, total commitment and long hours. Good examples of such roles are international assignments and operational experience.

22

IN FOCUS: THE CRITICAL JOB ASSIGNMENTS MODEL

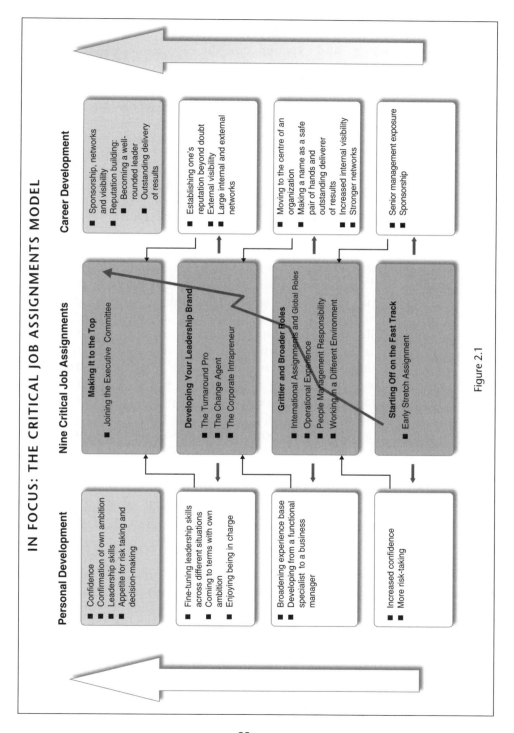

Personal Development

- Confidence
- Confirmation of own ambition
- Leadership skills
- Appetite for risk taking and decision-making

- Fine-tuning leadership skills across different situations
- Coming to terms with own ambition
- Enjoying being in charge

- Broadening experience base
- Developing from a functional specialist to a business manager

- Increased confidence
- More risk-taking

Nine Critical Job Assignments

Making It to the Top
- Joining the Executive Committee

Developing Your Leadership Brand
- The Turnaround Pro
- The Change Agent
- The Corporate Intrapreneur

Grittier and Broader Roles
- International Assignments and Global Roles
- Operational Experience
- People Management Responsibility
- Working in a Different Environment

Starting Off on the Fast Track
- Early Stretch Assignment

Career Development

- Sponsorship, networks and visibility
- Reputation building:
  - Becoming a well-rounded leader
  - Outstanding delivery of results

- Establishing one's reputation beyond doubt
- External visibility
- Large internal and external networks

- Moving to the centre of an organization
- Making a name as a safe pair of hands and outstanding deliverer of results
- Increased internal visibility
- Stronger networks

- Senior management exposure
- Sponsorship

Figure 2.1

23

They allow a woman to diversify her working style and build a broad base of knowledge and experience in the early days, which will act as a strong foundation for later senior management roles. These roles also provide a woman with project and change management skills, and improve her knowledge of business process improvement techniques, all of which she will have to build upon continually to help her make her name in one of these areas later. Gaining people management experience as early as possible also seems to be a big benefit. Motivating people, getting them behind ideas and galvanizing their talents and energies to deliver against increasingly challenging targets is a skill that is best learned and perfected early on. Many of the interviewees talked about how they could not have achieved some of their later challenges without a talented and dedicated team. As a woman approaches the end of her first career phase, settling down with a partner who is, and continues to be, utterly supportive of her career and regards it as being as important as his own, is crucial to her career success. Should babies arrive, taking no more than six months off for maternity leave and ideally staying in touch with the office while away will help her to demonstrate her continued commitment to her job. Returning to work full-time with an excellent support network in place is the next step. After the return from maternity leave she will have to prove that she is still committed to her role and reestablish herself as a high performer while at the same time ensuring she can fulfil her role as a mother. This is where the juggling starts. Senior sponsorship, taking new opportunities (to be combined with her childcare responsibilities) and resilience are important now. As she starts to hit the glass ceiling, outspiraling moves where she changes organization in the search for more senior roles will help her to overcome this barrier as well as further broadening her experience. Then comes the crunch point: the dual load of a demanding career and caring for a young family becomes too much and the superwoman needs a break. Many women take time out or a step back at this point. Many also leave the corporate world completely, but these women obviously do not feature in the research for this book. Once recharged after a break, women reenter the fast track and seek out more challenges. Drawing on sponsors and former bosses, they secure one or two high-powered roles, often in a global context. And then, as a woman approaches the later stages of her mid-career it comes along – the once-in-a-lifetime 'making your name' assignment: the one role that allows a woman to bring together everything she has learned up to that point, and that will establish her expertise and capability beyond any doubt within senior management circles and often far beyond. She builds a name for herself as a change agent, turnaround pro or corporate intrapreneur. And then there is the final push to the top as a member of the executive committee and then onward to become an executive or non-executive director.

As Figure 2.1 shows, there is no direct line to the top and not every woman even wants to make it there, nor does every man for that matter. In the majority of cases the road to the top is windy and includes occasional plateaus and a number of setbacks. None of the interviewees talked about a completely unimpeded and straight path to the top. Blocked promotions, side-steps to broaden the career base, possible redundancies and times of self-doubt are all part of a normal career path. And for many women there are the added hurdles of time out for maternity leave and possible periods of part-time working. Not every step outlined in Figure 2.1 was taken by all interviewees. In addition, the interviewees encountered the various elements set out in the model while on different paths. A number of the interviewees progressed to very senior roles in an agency or a consultancy firm before moving across to a senior role in a FTSE 100 company. Other interviewees had built a portfolio career with a number of very diverse roles before bringing it all together in one pivotal role and then progressing upward from there. Others again followed a more traditional general management or a more traditional functional career path. Some of the interviewees began their professional careers later, as they had taken time out to bring up their children, while others had delayed childbirth until their early forties.

As I have already mentioned, the critical job assignments model is not intended to act as a blueprint for how to move to the top; following an idealized sequence of events may mean missing out on many opportunities that present themselves along the way and may ultimately be counterproductive. Instead, the model tries to draw attention to the vital ingredients of successful careers for women: starting off on the fast track and obtaining senior management sponsorship, getting exposure to broad and gritty roles and gaining further in self-confidence, navigating the make-or-break years without coming off the fast track, making their name and standing out from the crowd, and finally breaking through the glass ceiling and making it to the top.

One last area that we need to look at is career planning. It is linked intrinsically with career phasing and career progression.

CAREER PLANNING

With only one exception, none of the interviewees had a career plan. One senior interviewee talked about the 'crazy paving' of careers. While they were clear about what they wanted in broad terms – for example, having children, working in a particular location, or working on the business side rather than as a specialist – none had a clear plan of how her career should unfold. Instead, they all had (and still have) a hunger to succeed, the readiness to seize opportunities with both hands, the energy to volunteer for additional responsibility and the courage to 'stick their necks out'. Only a handful of interviewees mentioned that it was their ambition and their competitive nature that drove them on. Passion, wanting to learn and getting bored with existing roles seem to be the main drivers for these women. They also talked about wanting to be good at what they do, which drove them on to deliver beyond expectations.

Interestingly, a significant number of the interviewees talked about having made it much further than they ever thought possible, and that they had not set out to become as senior as they were. A lack of role models or initial lack of self-confidence may have meant that aiming for the top was never regarded as a viable option. Only along the way did they realize that they had the skills, stamina and desire to go all the way to the top. A turning point for a number of the interviewees seems to have been the time when they first had the opportunity to make a significant business decision on their own, realizing that they were good at it and that they also enjoyed doing it. It was also often during this time that some of the interviewees realized that they were more ambitious than they had previously admitted to themselves. Ambition is not always regarded as an acceptable trait in women, and the interviewees' ambition may have been hidden until a pivotal event made them realize and acknowledge their true level of ambition, as the following quote shows: 'At that point I came to terms with my ambition. I really liked the role and thought, yes one day I may want to become the top person. This is fun' (Senior manager, FTSE 100 company).

The interviewees may not have had career plans, but many of them have sponsors and mentors, and are in touch with former bosses to discuss career opportunities. They also talked about how they carefully evaluated for its strategic value each new opportunity that presented itself. On the occasions when they felt they had not evaluated an opportunity carefully enough, they reported that, with hindsight, they should not have taken the role. A few of the most senior women also talked about how they had recently started to think much more consciously about how to make the next step to either an executive committee or a non-executive director (NED) position. Moving to these senior positions in an organization means breaking through the glass ceiling and therefore requires active planning. It may, however, also be a reflection of women entering the calmer, third phase of their careers, where careers become more planned once again. While they may not have had a textbook career plan, clearly none of the interviewees drifted in their careers. And that is not surprising. To be in the right place at the right time may require some luck, but above all it requires planning and preparation; the better prepared that people are, the luckier they appear to be. Also, given the additional hurdles that women face, having a clear view of where a woman wants to go and how to get there will significantly increase her chances of reaching her goal.

The benefits of career planning are widely recognized.[48,49,50,51] Taking action, setting priorities and making sure that opportunities are right for the individual and not the organization are best achieved once a plan is in place.[52] The intelligent career, introduced by Arthur and colleagues, and further developed by Jones and DeFillippi, sets out the six attributes a person requires to manage their own career successfully:[53,54] *know why* (values, attitudes and needs); *know how* (skills, knowledge, capabilities); *know whom* (networking and forming relationships with the right people); *know what* (opportunities, threats, requirements); *know where* (entering, training and advancing); and *know when* (timing of choices and activities). Adair stresses the importance of being prepared to meet challenges successfully and to make the most of them in terms of learning.[55] He points out that while it is rarely possible to understand exactly which challenges will be encountered in a career, if one looks far enough ahead and thinks about individual passions and talents, one can see what types of challenges may appeal and which are important to be prepared for. Career planning therefore becomes an important element of leadership development. Finally, Gallagher talks about the importance of 2–3-year plans and having an overall understanding of where one wants to go. Gallagher emphasizes the need to remain flexible within this plan, though, in order to adjust the next steps, go with the flow and be reminded that the next move may not necessarily be upward. Lateral moves are often good investments, to build a stronger foundation thus making oneself a strong candidate for that much desired senior management role.[56]

SUMMARY

Careers have become increasingly important for women, and the careers of successful women seem to fall broadly into three phases: first, high flyers who work hard and are in some cases even progressing faster than their male counterparts. When children arrive, which often happens in a woman's thirties, her toughest time begins, as this time also often coincides with laying the foundations for later senior management roles. Next, there is the juggling phase. While men progress upward unimpeded, women face difficult decisions, and those with children have to juggle demanding careers alongside motherhood. Ordering career and motherhood, making unplanned career moves and taking a step back or moving to the slower mommy track are often part of this middle phase. During the third phase of authentic contributors, things calm down and careers become more planned again. Across these three career phases, the nine different critical job assignments take place. They start off with an early stretch assignment, followed by broader and grittier roles such as international assignments and operational roles. Then women set about making their name as change agent, turnaround pros or intrapreneurs. This is followed by the final push to the top to join an executive committee or become an executive or non-executive director. Career planning is an important element in increasing the odds of achieving one's career goals. While the interviewees in this study did not have concrete career plans, they all had sponsors, were open to new opportunities and evaluated each one carefully for its strategic importance. A passion for learning and intellectual curiosity drove them on. Despite a lack of a formal career plan, these attributes have allowed them to be in the right place at the right time.

3

BEING SELECTED FOR CRITICAL JOB ASSIGNMENTS

Being good puts you on the starting line. To win the Grand Prix you need your network.

(Paola Cuneo, General Manager, BT)

If you don't blow your own trumpet, nobody will do it for you.

(Senior Manager, FTSE 100 Company)

Most of us know relatively little about the decision-making processes that go on when senior managers decide whom to promote or whom to select for a crucial assignment. This is not surprising, as many decision-makers are probably not even fully aware themselves of all the reasons for making their decisions. Biases in decision-making are rarely overt and we are often not aware of how our own deeply held prejudices influence our decisions and actions on a daily basis. In an ideal world, all roles would be advertised widely and contain clearly specified success criteria, which would then be assessed consistently at the selection stage. The process would be completely transparent, objective and fair to all. However, this is not always the case in reality, and while good selection processes and training help to make the overall process fairer and more objective, best practice is not always in place. Furthermore, the more senior an appointment, the more subjective the selection criteria become and the fewer objective selection tools, such as reasoning tests or work simulation exercises, are routinely used.

Ruderman and colleagues examined a wide range of decision-making parameters as part of an in-depth study of just under 40 professionals.[1] While the findings overall showed more similarities than differences between the men and women in the sample, there were some noteworthy variations. When senior recruiting managers talked about why they had chosen a particular male candidate, they frequently mentioned that they felt reassured and comfortable that the person would be able to do the job. Furthermore, the desire to retain a talented person who was available as a result of the return from an overseas assignment or after the sale of a division was mentioned much more frequently for men than for women. On the other hand, personal strengths were frequently referred to as a reason for promotion for women. Senior executives were more likely to promote a woman into a role that was similar to her existing position, and continuity was a frequently cited reason for the promotion. Another reason mentioned was that a woman had asked for the promotion. This was often the case where a woman had initially been given a lower-level role to prove her abilities, and after becoming impatient she requested her promised promotion and the manager yielded. This was much less often the case for men, who were less frequently requested to serve a trial period at a lower level. Finally, equal opportunity and diversity considerations were mentioned as a reason for a promotion decision, but much more frequently in the case of women. These findings highlight subtle and deeply-ingrained role stereotypes in operation when senior managers make and later justify their recruitment decisions.

Some promotions are significant step changes and the new responsibilities are very different from those a person might have undertaken in the past.[2] The promotion decision is therefore often difficult as decision-makers have not seen the person under consideration working in the job in question.[3,4] It is in these uncertain situations, where there is a lack of information, that subjectivity and gut instinct are more likely to surface. People generally feel more comfortable with others who think, behave and generally are like them, and as senior men still make the majority of promotion decisions into senior roles, this desire for social similarity disadvantages women. In a poll of over 800 US voters, 51 percent of men and women commented that they would feel very comfortable with a female CEO of a large US corporation. While voters listed a number of advantages that they expected female power to bring to large corporations, such as family-friendly policies, more effective downsizing decisions, and more trustworthy and values-oriented leadership, many felt that women would lack the toughness expected in a CEO.[5] In a number of different studies, Catalyst, a US-based organization supporting the advancement of women, found that the characteristics of the ideal worker that are mentioned most frequently are assertiveness, independence, results-orientation and being a good problem-solver – terms usually associated with men.[6] Another barrier for the promotion of women to senior roles is that there are still only so few of them in senior roles. This means that each appointment at this level becomes highly visible and is therefore a much riskier appointment for the senior decision-maker who makes it.[7] Other factors that are likely to influence a decision-maker are personal networks and endorsement through mentors, which, as we shall see in the following sections, are criteria that again tend not to work in women's favor.[8]

THE IMPORTANCE OF NETWORKS

To become a leader involves being chosen or identified as one by others, and for this to happen hard work and meritocracy are not enough. Without connections to the inner circle of senior managers, or at least representation in the inner circle, this leadership endorsement will not take place because those in charge will not be aware of a person's achievements.[9] Networks are important, as everyone relies on others to provide vital information, support, practical help and feedback. People cannot operate in isolation, and trying to go it alone is rarely successful. In addition to women receiving information from their networks, these also help to build a woman's reputation and pass news of her personal achievements to others. Interestingly, the majority of the interviewees in this study described themselves as not being good at networking. When they talked about the type of networking they do, they referred to building and maintaining one-to-one relationships much more than making use of traditional group networking events. They stay in touch with colleagues or with former bosses as an informal support network, and use this as one of their main career progression aids. A number of the interviewees talked about the acceleration benefits of spending some time in roles with organizations outside the corporate mainstream, such as industry or government bodies, which provided access to many influential senior contacts. One senior woman, for example, talked about the benefits she gained from working for a not-for-profit government agency during a secondment. This allowed her to widen her network to include important government contacts as well as senior people from many different organizations and industry sectors. She said: 'I wish I had had this role 10 years ago. If you are junior it is difficult to make good senior contacts and a role like this really helps' (Senior manager, FTSE 100 company).

Networks fulfill various functions for women. They provide information about available job opportunities, visibility, information about unwritten rules, and access to senior decision-makers. They are also important for senior decision-makers, who use them to validate a candidate's standing in the organization; being a member of a powerful and influential network indicates that the candidate is also powerful and influential.[10]

Access to job opportunities

Many roles are not advertised and instead are filled informally. Interesting roles that are often high-profile or urgent demand a safe pair of hands and these are often filled by people who are known to the senior decision-makers and who have proved themselves in the past. The old boys' network is the term routinely given to the process of men getting jobs through their network of other male colleagues. And there is a lot of evidence that this old boys' network works for men. Davidson and Cooper, for example, found that over half of senior management jobs are filled via personal contacts with other senior men.[11] Women also find new roles through their networks. Significant numbers of the interviewees talked about getting new roles by staying in touch with bosses who had moved up in their careers and who were now looking for a trusted pair of hands to help them make their own new job a success. But there is also some evidence that the jobs women secure through their networks are less senior and less well paid than those secured by men through *their* networks, because women tend to network with other women who themselves tend to be in more junior, less well-paid and less influential roles.[12]

Access to unwritten rules

Every organization has unwritten rules, the kind of information that is vital to operating successfully in an organization but which cannot be found in a company brochure or on the company's website: Who is important and wields power but is not easily recognizable as a power broker on the organization chart? What behaviors are truly valued by the senior management team, and how to get the promotion you have been seeking? While open and transparent rules for promotion are one of the recommendations for increasing women's chances of progression, women can also help themselves by overcoming their concerns about getting to grips with unwritten rules.[13] For most roles there are many capable applicants, and the person who gets the role may not always be the best qualified. Adhering to unwritten rules and meeting hidden expectations are powerful decision-making criteria. The lack of access to this important information can seriously impair a person's promotion prospects. It is an organization's senior leadership that sends subtle yet powerful signals to the rest of the organization about which behaviors and values are truly valued and respected, irrespective of what the company literature says. Almost three-quarters of a Catalyst study's respondents named, in order of frequency, using their networks, observing others, advice from mentors, asking for personal feedback, and often plain trial and error as their strategies to learn about unwritten rules in organizations.[14] Interviewees mentioned the importance of networking both within and outside the organization as an important element to advancing in a career. Over half mentioned the importance of being visible, and just under half talked about the importance of promoting yourself and your work.

Women's exclusion from powerful networks

To gain access to information about jobs, unwritten rules and senior managers, women need to be part of not just any network, but of powerful networks. As we tend to interact more easily with those with whom we share many similarities, women tend to network with women and men with men. Furthermore, strong endorsements from powerful sponsors in senior management positions are more frequently available to men than to women. Because of the potential for sexual power imbalances, it has been suggested that women are less likely to have senior male sponsors and mentors, and therefore have fewer endorsements.[15]

The consequences of women's exclusion from powerful male networks is further exacerbated through an increased reliance on 'who you know' strategies as organizations get flatter.[16] A head-hunter talks about women's networking ghettos:

> You have to be comfortable networking with men otherwise you end up in female networking ghettos. Women are often not good at getting hooked into efficient networks ... Sometimes women are also not visible because they are not in the right role in an

organization or in the right organization. (Mary Lawrance, Owner, Cariance Executive Search and Consulting)

Women need to put themselves on the radar. Being in a department that is central to the organization will improve a woman's visibility, make her more likely to be noticed as an important contributor and therefore attract the attention of those who can influence her career.[17]

ASKING FOR PROMOTION

At the end of the 1970s, Hennig and Jardim reported that women have to feel fully competent in their current job before they believe they are ready to move on to the next level in the organization.[18] Men, on the other hand, apparently took every reasonable opportunity to progress upward. More than thirty years on and things do not seem to have changed much. Women are still less likely to put themselves forward for promotion than men.[19] When women evaluate job advertisements they look for a much higher overlap between required skills and their own skills than men do before they apply for the role. A study at Hewlett Packard (HP) showed that women only applied for a promotion if they thought they met 100 percent of the criteria, whereas men applied if they thought they met 60 percent. A study at Lloyds TSB showed that, while women meet and exceed targets, they do not tend to apply for promotion.[20] In addition to senior male managers making assumptions about what types of assignments women may want, and what they are capable of doing, women's own reluctance to put themselves forward for promotions often exacerbates the problem.[21] Women do not seem to be asking for promotion as actively as men. Instead, they wait for their achievements to be recognized by their line manager and to be rewarded with a promotion.[22] Women's own beliefs about their capabilities seem to have an impact on how they react to job opportunities in their work environment.

Asking for promotion is not too dissimilar to negotiating a pay rise. Both are about asking for more. Linda Babcock and her colleagues present an interesting set of studies which explore men's and women's tendencies to negotiate.[23] In the first study, they found that the starting salary of female MBA graduates was 7.6 percent lower than that of similar male MBA graduates. While 57 percent of male MBA students tried to negotiate the offered starting salary, only 7 percent of the female students did so. In a follow-on study, students were offered between $3 and $10 to take part in an experiment. When students were given $3 at the end of the experiment, men asked for more money nine times more often than the women did. Finally, in an online survey, men reported that they take part in negotiations more frequently than did women. The authors go on to point out that, while women have often been taught not to negotiate there is evidence that women's attitudes to negotiating can be reversed when they learn how important it is.

IN FOCUS: RISK-TAKING

Are women ready for early stretch assignments and for an accelerated career progression? More generally, are they ready to take risks throughout their careers? Women are usually seen as risk-averse. Traditional risk-taking studies that use simulation scenarios involving portfolio investment decisions confirm this view. When women were asked what percentage of a certain amount of money they would invest in a new venture with unlimited potential reward but a highly uncertain outcome, the majority tended to be willing to invest less than 50 percent of the money which put them into the risk-averse group.[24] Maxfield and colleagues[25] stepped outside these hypothetical investment scenarios and examined women's risk-taking behavior in the context of real work settings in a study of over 650 professional women in the USA. They asked the participants to indicate the frequency with which they had engaged in 'business/professional opportunities, whose success is not assured, that require learning by doing, and where [you] have to take personal responsibility for failures on the way' (p. 589). The research team deliberately avoided the use of such terminology as 'risk' and 'risky'. The results showed that the respondents, all well-educated professional women who were taking part in a leadership development conference, readily embraced risks. About half of the respondents indicated that they frequently took on major investment decisions, major business development opportunities, major advocacy positions and major business relationships. Furthermore, at least three-quarters of the respondents agreed that they took on opportunities to run new programmes, take on a new job or take on a change initiative.

The study found that the desire to make an impact, a belief in one's ability to succeed and access to professional networks to validate one's thinking were strong motivators to take risks. Maxfield and her colleagues suggest a number of interesting ideas as to why women might be seen as being less risk-embracing than men. First, as women are seen stereotypically as being risk-averse, any risk-taking behavior is not noticed. People only see what they are looking for. Second, women may find it more difficult to talk about their risk-taking because self-promotion is not considered acceptable behavior for women and is often regarded as bragging. As we shall see later in this chapter, women tend to use 'we' when they talk about their successes as a way of overcoming negative reactions to self-promotion. As a result, women's own risk-taking may not be seen as an individual effort, but rather as the work of a team. Women find themselves in a double bind – they either follow society's expectations of being risk-averse or they break this stereotype by taking risks, and as a consequence have their values and motives questioned. Finally, asking questions and validating one's own thinking by turning to one's networks may be seen as timidity and a lack of decisiveness rather than as a valid way to contextualize risk. Maxfield and her co-workers suggest a number of different strategies for women to make their own risk-taking more visible. First, they advise using the language of risk and presenting clear cost–benefit calculations; second, they advocate sharing personal achievements, including how a woman has dealt successfully with uncertain situations, and how she has taken calculated risks. Third, when women tap into their networks they need to make it clear that they are seeking information and not a decision; women need to clarify that they are the ultimate decision-maker in the process. Finally, Maxfield and colleagues recommend working with people who are seen as risk-takers in order to gain access to projects that allow a woman to demonstrate her readiness and ability to take calculated risks.

Clearly, a fair degree of risk-taking is vital to career success. Risk-aversion has been targeted as one of the reasons why women do not progress to senior management roles.[26] Many of the most senior women who took part in the study that underpins this book talked about the need for more risk-taking among women. In their view, women have to be ready to 'put their heads above the parapet'. Early risk-taking and learning from failure are advocated. Gallagher talks about the 'paradoxical value of failure': risk-taking increases the likelihood of failure, and failure helps us to learn.[27] One of the interviewees echoed this point by saying 'I have learnt the most from the biggest disasters.' Risk-taking is a sign of the most effective form of taking action and being in control. The courage to seek out challenging roles takes a woman out of her comfort zone. It is not about ignoring one's doubts and fears but instead about being aware of these feelings and harnessing them to enable the taking of calculated risks, and making plans of how to overcome these fears.[28]

Outspiraling moves

Women tend to get ahead faster by making so-called outspiraling moves, a term that refers to moving to a new company in response to blocked career progression. The importance for women of outspiraling moves or lateral transfers into leadership positions has been noted in different places.[29] There is also evidence of this career strategy in the group of women interviewed for this book. A significant number had obtained senior roles by leaving their organization. One senior manager explains why outspiraling moves may benefit women:

If people are in a company for a long time they become 'in awe' of seniority; they get scared of being on the executive. Moving around has helped me and I have progressed faster. Social capital matters less when you are moving around. Men are more visionary and less incremental. I have not had a career plan but I have learnt something new from every role. You need to have the big picture on every job: 'Where can I contribute most and where can I learn most?' Think about roles first, then the stripes. Above all strive to work with people with whom you can be yourself, in order to best deliver in the role. (Amanda MacKenzie, Group Marketing Director, Aviva)

There is a glass ceiling. I have always asked myself 'Do I move sideways or do I leave?' I have always left in those situations. (Sophie Turner Laing, Managing Director, Entertainment and News, British Sky Broadcasting)

THE ACCEPTABILITY OF SELF-PROMOTION

Self-promotion is something that women are always advised to do more of: 'Tell others about your achievements', 'Use every opportunity and don't hold back', 'Don't wait for others to recognize and reward your achievements, as they won't'. We hear about it again and again, but so many women still keep quiet or feel uncomfortable when they talk about their achievements. They feel it is bragging and something that 'the guys' do. Women's gender-role stereotyping seems to have remained powerful over the decades. Self-promotion is one of the traits that is seen as unfeminine, and women who show this trait overtly are being ostracized. Peggy Klaus calls it the daily 'tug-of-war between showing humility and showcasing personal accomplishments' (p. 332).[30] She also outlines just how damaging it is not to let others know about your achievements because it affects access to promotion, salary increases, high visibility projects and many daily negotiations over work matters. While women wait for their supervisors to recognize their achievements and reward them with a deserved promotion, in the absence of being told about what women expect, managers often make their own assumptions about what a woman may or may not want. As a result, women are often overlooked for interesting job assignments or promotion. Esther Schindler talks about the importance of self-promotion and the need to be confident about putting yourself forward for promotion to the next level. Women self-impose a glass ceiling by being too timid and afraid to leave their comfort zone to take on a big new challenge. Being proactive about looking for opportunities is always more rewarding than waiting for others to offer them. Dudley and Goodson's study of almost 20,000 professionals from 34 countries showed that women are more reluctant to talk about their achievements than are men.[31] The authors point out that promoting your own achievements is part and parcel of a modern career management strategy. While delivering outstanding results is the number one priority, letting others know about these achievements is also important. When the interviewees in my study were asked how they had talked about their achievements without it coming across as bragging, their advice was to talk about the team's achievements rather than personal achievements; less 'I' and more 'we' was the general consensus. One senior woman talked about the advantage of working on a number of interesting, high-profile projects that people wanted to hear about. She explained how she had used both internal and external forums to talk about the projects and her achievements. A number of the interviewees also talked about the power of external media coverage of personal achievements, which can help to build a reputation more widely. The interviewees agreed that waiting for others to recognize good work is just not realistic in the modern workplace. Bosses are too busy to always fully understand what everyone in the team is doing. Without attention being drawn toward them, achievements can go unnoticed. Wendy Kinney talks about the importance of the 'elevator pitch'.[32] When you meet someone senior, be ready to talk about what you are doing in an engaging and impactful manner in a few sentences. This is a very effective way to make sure that the time spent with a senior colleague is well used. Being able to talk about a current project engagingly rather than merely saying 'All is going well; I am busy' gives the other person more information on which to further build a conversation.

TAKING CHARGE

Taking action is a concept that emerges routinely in studies about successful women. It is also referred to as *agency* and is particularly important when it comes to the selection process. Putting yourself forward for roles, communicating your desire to move up, and using existing connections to find out about new and interesting roles are crucial in order to secure a new role. However, taking action is often deemed to be a male characteristic. While men tend to plan more, compete vigorously for the next level and are confident about putting themselves forward for new roles, women tend to prefer lateral moves, personal growth and cooperation.[33]

In a study of over 500 male and female middle managers in a range of organizations in Australia, Wood and Lindorff examined the possible impact on their promotion-seeking behaviors of men's and women's gender and social roles.[34] While there were no gender differences in how male and female managers perceived available progression opportunities in their organizations, or the extent to which they aspired to move to senior management positions, a number of other interesting differences emerged. First, male middle managers expected to achieve promotion to senior management more often than did their female colleagues. Furthermore, men and women mentioned different reasons for their career success to date. While women were much more likely to put their most recent promotion down to individual qualities, such as mentoring relationships, personality and the potential for development, men were much more likely to attribute their previous promotion to outcomes such as experience, and in particular to the range and length of that experience. Finally, when asked for reasons why a future promotion might not be achieved, more women reported a lack of personal interest, family reasons and negative stereotyping, while men more frequently reported politics, personal inadequacies or a lack of opportunity. Therefore, women's own perceptions of what is important for their career development may influence their promotion-seeking behavior, unduly emphasizing interdependence and cooperation as desirable behaviors and neglecting the more competitive and outcome-focused behaviors used by men.

GETTING CRITICAL JOB ASSIGNMENTS

Detailed information about how the interviewees got their assignments is available for 41 of the 112 critical job assignments the interviewees talked about. In 36 percent of cases the interviewees reported that they were approached by someone more senior in the organization and offered the role; 17 percent of the women had proactively approached their boss and asked for a new challenge or a specific role; 29 percent went either through a formal external or internal selection process or were head-hunted, which was followed by a formal selection process; 10 percent were approached by contacts outside the organization; and the remaining 8 percent of critical job assignments were obtained either through project staffing or being a member of a high-potential pool. These statistics show how important are both relationships and taking charge of one's own career. There were no recognizable differences across assignments. A number of interviewees mentioned that, apart from their first one or two roles, they never again applied for jobs and instead were always approached by others offering new work opportunities.

SUMMARY

Selection decisions are often influenced by subtle personal biases that work against women, such as the desire for similarity and the reluctance to make highly visible assignments because of the increased scrutiny attracted by such decisions.

Networks are central to obtaining a promotion or a new assignment as they provide information about job opportunities, access to senior people, information about an organization's unwritten rules, and visibility. But these benefits are only available from the right types of network: those that include senior decision-makers and those that are regarded as powerful and influential. Women do not always have easy access to such networks, which have on occasion been called 'the old boys' network'. Women also do not actively describe themselves as good networkers.

In addition to being part of the right networks, women need to ask more proactively for promotions or new challenges, which many studies show that they still do not do in many cases. Instead, they wait for others to recognize and reward their achievements, a strategy that is not viable in a busy work environment, where managers often do not have time to understand what everyone in the wider team is achieving. The data from the interviews reinforces the importance of asking proactively for assignments and using one's networks, as the majority of assignments were obtained either through a woman's network or by asking for them. Furthermore, to get the attention of those who have influence over their careers, women have to be proactive about talking about their achievements. They, however, face the stigma of being self-promoting, a behavior that is not seen as acceptable for women. Talking about one's team's rather than about one's personal achievements is the way that the interviewees have got around this problem. Taking charge is a central theme in this chapter, which also applies to leaving an organization and looking for new opportunities elsewhere if career aspirations are blocked in a woman's current position. These outspiraling moves are important for women, to enable them to break through the glass ceiling.

PART II

4

THE EARLY STRETCH ASSIGNMENT: STARTING OFF ON THE FAST TRACK

Pick up a project and run with it. Grab it with both hands and manage it efficiently.

(Claire Jenkins, Group Director, Corporate Affairs, Rexam)

It is better to have a small project but to own it than to be a player on a big project. If you own a project it makes you more memorable as the results are attributable to you.

(Wendy Antaw, Head of Information Systems, Land Securities Group)

A challenging assignment early in a woman's career is particularly important. Not only does it allow her to be noted as a potential future leader, it also allows the woman to build up her confidence, which is one of the most important elements of ongoing career success. Being completely out of one's depth technically, building credibility with established experts, taking on significant responsibility and working with the senior management team are some of the defining characteristics of early stretch assignments. They are often encountered as part of smaller, under-resourced organizations or departments at times of high demand where it is an 'all hands to the pump' situation and a young woman gets opportunities which go far beyond her level of experience.

My training in a small boutique law firm in London ... a corporate law firm ... I was working 24/7. There were two to three all-nighters per week. It was at the height of the M&A [mergers and acquisitions] activity. We had to turn up in front of all the senior partners twice a week at 7.30am or 8am ... articles were distributed shortly beforehand ... up to 50 pages per article. Anyone could be asked to talk to any of these articles. You had to have the confidence to stand up and speak. Sometimes I turned it around and said 'I have only been here for 4 months, this is my understanding, I would value your view.' I asked questions and at times I would say 'I don't know' … Honesty and speaking my mind in front of senior partners gained me respect. The other trainees were a support network. We all stayed in the same house. There was humour at the end of a very long day. We developed good, close relationships and got to know each other well. There was no competition. I am still in touch with some of them now. (Senior manager, FTSE 100 company)

These early opportunities with access to senior managers act as an accelerator allowing women to skip a number of steps and progress through the early phases of their careers much faster than their peers. Once they have come to the attention of senior managers, other high-profile projects tend to follow. If a woman continues to deliver to expectations, is prepared to take on bigger and grittier roles, and puts in maximum commitment, her career often stays on an accelerated trajectory. And as we saw in Chapter 2, fast career progression seems to be a prerequisite for making it to the top.

Strictly speaking, all the job assignments discussed in this book represent a stretch and are therefore stretch assignments. The unique characteristic of the early stretch assignment, as the title suggests, lies in its timing and the occurrence of the challenges associated with working on a stretching project early in one's career. Early stretch assignments have been shown to be the foundation of many successful careers. Cox and Cooper's review of the literature suggests that people who have built successful careers often obtained roles with high levels of responsibility early in their career.[1] Their own study of high flyers further confirms these findings. Their interviewees, often at managing director level, reported the defining features of their early assignments to be high levels of responsibility coupled with little support – a 'sink or swim' assignment. In a follow-on investigation, White and colleagues found that, of the 48 successful women they interviewed, a third described an early challenge in their careers as one of their significant career events.[2] In addition to being able to demonstrate to others what they can do, this challenge allowed women to show themselves what they were capable of and increased their confidence to seek more challenging roles. As we shall see below, the findings of the study that underpins this book offer a further corroboration of these earlier studies.

The human resources (HR) director of a large FTSE 100 company shared a recent experience about young women's appetite for early stretch assignments. A role had become available in the organization as part of a maternity cover arrangement, and the HR director offered all graduate trainees the post as an early stretch assignment. It was in an area in which none of the trainees was qualified and involved daily access to one of the senior managers of the organization. None of the female graduate trainees were interested in the role. They had all already found their first follow-on jobs in the organization through their own networks; however, the roles they had secured involved less responsibility and less contact with senior people than the post on offer. The women felt that the maternity cover role would take them off the path they had mapped out for themselves, which they thought would get them to their desired dream role eventually. The HR director felt that the women had limited themselves by aiming for smaller, incremental career steps.

The roles the interviewees talked about as their early stretch assignment are varied, appearing in the form of early strategy consulting assignments, training in small firms during boom times, or the first role straight out of training. The challenges associated with these roles are significant, but so is the learning, as we shall see in the next few sections.

JOB-SPECIFIC CHALLENGES

The interviewees mentioned four different types of job-specific challenges: being out of your depth; working with senior managers for the first time; building credibility; and learning about the organization and about yourself.

Out of your depth

There is a lot of new learning that has to take place at the start of every new role. Not without reason do we allow a new job incumbent some time to settle in. With early stretch assignments this learning is intensified as the role is often in a completely unfamiliar environment for which no previous training has been provided. A number of the interviewees talked about the challenges they had encountered as part of early strategy consulting roles, where every project is in a different industry sector, every problem is intellectually different, and steep learning curves are part of day-to-day life:

> This role was a big stretch. I didn't know what people were talking about ... IT people like to show off and show that others don't know the issues. I had to pretend that I had knowledge where I had none. . At the beginning I hated IT. I thought I would never learn it. I didn't show enough self-confidence. (Hana Rolles, Head of Online Marketing and Sales, Vodafone Group)

Dealing with difficult people and situations, either in the form of people management, stakeholder management or negotiations, also made the women feel out of their depth. One senior manager in the finance industry recalls her early stretch assignment:

> I had two staff reporting to me and one was underperforming. I had to manage her underperformance and eventually to sack her. There was lots of self-reflection. 'Am I doing the right thing?' Everyone was watching to see the outcome. Fear makes you want to achieve the best possible outcome. (Senior manager, finance industry)

Dotlich and colleagues talk about 'common hurts' during a stretch assignment.[3] These are the times when people realize they are making mistakes, or that they do not understand a situation. One of these hurts is realizing that one does not have the necessary knowledge. Becoming aware of this lack of knowledge and acknowledging it is the first step to turning an early stretch assignment into a developmental experience. Openness to the new experience, experimenting with new ways of working, and finding various routes to acquiring new knowledge (by listening, observing or asking, for example) are other important lessons that women take away from this assignment, as we shall see in the Lessons Learned section later in the chapter.

Working with senior managers

One of the main challenges, and arguably also one of the main benefits, of the early stretch assignment, is the interaction with senior managers. The interviewees talked about working with a senior manager on a consulting assignment, discussing cases with a partner in a small law firm, or reporting to a group HR director about process inefficiencies as examples of such senior management interactions. It is all about learning how to interact effectively with people at the very top of the organization, understanding their way of thinking, working to their priorities, delivering to their expectations and finding the confidence to speak up and share one's views as a young woman in the company of mainly men who are 20 and 30 years older. A middle manager remembered her early assignment:

> The senior stakeholders were generally very open and willing to work with me but sometimes they had no time and would say 'What are you doing here? It is not the time to discuss this now.' I thought that they did not want to work with me any more but I realized that it was only a timing issue and I learned to respect that. (Middle manager, FTSE 100 company)

> An early stretch assignment gives you exposure and allows you to develop your political antennae. You cannot throw your weight around at senior management level; you need to learn to build consensus and coalitions. It requires emotional intelligence. The way of working at senior level is different to how you work at junior level. It is a great exposure even if it is only for three months. (Human resources director, FTSE 100 company)

Building credibility

Building credibility is a theme we shall encounter as part of a number of different job assignments described in this book. Building credibility in the context of an early stretch assignment is probably one of the toughest situations. The women are usually younger than their colleagues and stakeholders, often significantly so. They have comparatively little industry and technical knowledge, and are often put in situations where they have to gain the cooperation of others without having any formal authority. Their recommendations are often dismissed by subject matter experts and senior managers before they have even been presented. In these situations, women have little or no track record to build on, few contacts to draw on for support, and little experience of how to operate effectively in a large organization. Often, all that remains for a woman to fall back on are her interpersonal skills and personal strengths, such as analytical thinking, persuasion and tenacity.

Learning about the organization and about yourself

In addition to learning about a challenging role, young women have to learn about the wider context in which they are operating:

> I didn't know how the organization works ... finance, sales, the construction department ... what are the different people doing, what are the company's drivers? I had to gain business acumen at the same time as learning about the role. It took some time. I asked lots of questions, I was watching and observing and spent quite a bit of time on site to gain first-hand experience. (Emma Cariaga, Head of Strategic Projects, Land Securities Group)

And it is not only the organization that has to be decoded. Women have to learn about themselves and about how to operate effectively in organizations. It is about finding a style that works for both themselves and the organization:

> You have to develop a style and personality that allows you to relate well to others, such as peers, juniors and seniors, so they speak well of you. You have to learn to give and take. Don't just be brutally competitive otherwise everyone dislikes you. You need to find an acceptable form of competition. (Alison Carnwath, Chairman, Land Securities Group)

Many of the women mentioned the lack of role models throughout their careers, which has made it difficult for them to find good guides to ways of operating effectively as a woman in an organization. We shall hear more about the importance of role models in the In Focus box in Chapter 7. As a result of this absence of role models, women have to experiment, and learn by trial and error. They have to learn to tread a fine line: being feminine enough so as not to alienate others by not conforming to expectations, but being masculine enough to be able to mix with 'the boys' and fit in.

A number of the interviewees talked about their journey of self-discovery before they arrived at a style that allowed them to be effective and respected but still maintained their sense of self.

WOMEN-SPECIFIC CHALLENGES

Building credibility in a male-dominated environment

Being a woman in a male-dominated world brings additional hurdles, and these may seem particularly daunting for a woman at the start of her career as she may not by then have found techniques to overcome them. Some of these techniques may be learned as part of that first stretch assignment. As mentioned earlier in the chapter, building credibility is one of the big challenges for women during an early stretch assignment, and building credibility as a young woman among older men is particularly difficult, which the following quotes illustrate:

> People are more inclined to take men seriously, and women have to work a bit harder to convince others that they have a good point to make. A lot of organizations are dominated by men who want to put their best foot forward, whereas women just want to do a good job and expect a promotion to come through. It is harder for a woman to slot into that pattern of male behavior and to prove herself. (Senior manager, FTSE 100 company)

> I was working as a young consultant ... with people who were 20 years older than me and who had been in the company for a long time. I had to try to have gravitas and credibility and get people to listen to what I had to say. (Senior manager, FTSE 100 company)

> Senior management is very male-dominated ... there are not many women in senior roles. I faced resistance about being a young woman. Most of my stakeholders were male and in their forties and fifties. My stakeholders perceived me as not being able to add value. (Middle manager, FTSE 100 company)

LESSONS LEARNED

There are three main lessons women take away from their early stretch assignment: self-confidence, gaining a senior management perspective, and developing emotional intelligence; all are important foundations for future senior management roles.

Self-confidence

The most fundamental take-away lesson from an early stretch assignment is self-confidence – the confidence that one can operate successfully in unfamiliar situations and can add value despite the lack of technical expertise:

> If you persevere you can learn anything and handle anything. If you apply common sense you can succeed in a new area and solve problems. You need to portray confidence. This has paid off throughout my career … You can tackle anything and add value to anything even if you are not an expert. (Hana Rolles, Head of Online Marketing and Sales, Vodafone Group)

> It has allowed me to become more confident. It has shown me that even if it seems really difficult, if I try I can overcome it (Senior manager, FTSE 100 company)

Another element of confidence that early stretch assignments bring is the confidence that it is possible to work with senior managers. It demystifies working with such managers and allows women to realize that they can work at that level on a daily basis. Preparation is important, and so is understanding how to present information and how to engage at this level. The early exposure provides security and removes the fear of working with the most senior people in an organization. One middle manager of a FTSE 100 company recalled learning that senior managers are also human.

Self-confidence is vital to women progressing to senior roles and, in addition to an early stretch assignment, two other critical assignments during a woman's career also seem to act as effective confidence boosters: creating something new (see Chapter 9) and joining the executive committee (see Chapter 12). The In Focus section in Chapter 9 takes a closer look at this important personal attribute. Finally, a successful early stretch assignment that has further increased a woman's self-confidence is likely also to increase her appetite for taking a risk and taking on more stretching assignments in the future.

Gaining a senior management perspective

In addition to gaining the confidence to interact with senior managers, working with people at this level in the organization allows young women to obtain an insight into their way of thinking and operating. Which issues are important, and which are not? Which skills are valued in the organization, and which not? Which approaches are effective, and which are not?

> I have gained a top management perspective ... I have learned what is not important – don't be too detailed, as people don't care ... I learned not to dwell on detail. (Hana Rolles, Head of Online Marketing and Sales, Vodafone Group)

> I heard my boss talk about others and learned what was valued and what wasn't. (Senior manager, FTSE 100 company)

Learning how to think like senior managers helps younger managers to understand the deliverables that are valued and what styles are effective. This in turn helps them to be seen as effective performers and to build a reputation as someone with potential.

Developing emotional intelligence

Learning to work effectively with others is about more than finding the right style though, and goes much deeper. It is about developing a real understanding of others and their motives, views and concerns. Women have to learn to persuade, to manage conflict and to overcome resistance. To do this successfully, a true understanding of the other person involved is critical.

> To persuade people ... you need to know subtleties of what people want and what they are interested in. You need to understand what pushes people's buttons. (Emma Cariaga, Head of Strategic Projects, Land Securities Group)

> I learned to understand different people by listening ... Trust your intuition and don't be too critical of yourself. Know that people are motivated by different things. You need people to back you and sponsor you. (HR director, FTSE 100 company)

Understanding yourself and others is part of emotional intelligence, which Daniel Goleman defines as 'the capacity for recognizing our own feelings and those of others, for motivating ourselves, and for managing emotions well in ourselves and in our relationships' (p. 317).[4]

He points to research by David McClelland which shows that emotional intelligence is a better predictor of star performance than IQ. A lack of emotional intelligence has repeatedly been shown to be a derailer for senior managers.[5,6]

CAREER BENEFITS

Career acceleration through senior sponsorship

Working successfully with senior managers on high-profile assignments early in their careers allows women to appear on the high-potential radar. This helps them to gain sponsorship from senior managers, which is a career accelerator that is hard to match and allows them to skip some of the more junior steps of their careers and move more quickly to meatier, grittier roles.

IN FOCUS: SPONSORS

During the interviews sponsors emerged as important and powerful people in women's careers. Almost all the interviewees talked about how important sponsors had been for their careers. A sponsor is a person who is senior and well-connected in the organization where the woman works. Former bosses or project leaders often become sponsors. They have seen a woman perform exceptionally well in a role, have recognized her future potential, and as a result are now opening up new opportunities for her. An important characteristic of sponsors is their belief in the abilities of their protégées. The data from the interviews also indicates that sponsors move women on to the next challenge, often earlier than the women would have chosen to do so themselves. A female CEO, for example, recalls how petrified she was about a number of new opportunities her sponsors had suggested to her. Without their encouragement she would not have looked for challenges of that magnitude at that point in time. Finally, sponsors encourage women to aim high. One senior manager described how her mentor, a well-known person in her industry, painted a picture of a whole new world for her. He allowed her to dream and imagine a completely different level of achievement, something she felt was completely out of her reach. He opened it up and said: 'Just imagine. Why not?'

Sponsors talk about their protégées and their successes in senior circles, put them forward for promotion and suggest them for projects that are important for the organization. They open doors and vouch for the quality of the work their protégée will deliver. Via a sponsor, women often find an accelerated path through the organization. Sponsorship may sound like cronyism to some, and a small number of the middle managers I interviewed for this study insisted on progressing on merit alone. It is important to note, though, that women with sponsors are not promoted solely because of their connections. Committed sponsors and subsequent career opportunities only come to those women who consistently deliver excellent work, who demonstrate maximum commitment and who are known to be open to new challenges. A sponsor simply provides a way to gain visibility in senior circles. The interviewees mentioned that when it comes to staffing new projects they themselves automatically think of people they know personally or whom they have heard about through other senior colleagues. As sponsors are central to a woman's career it is important to be aware of who could be a potential sponsor. One interviewee talked about career stakeholders rather than sponsors, and about being aware of who are the most influential people for one's career. These people must be kept up to date with one's achievements and progress.

While some sponsors may support a woman's career for a long period of time, others may become less important and less influential over time, and new advocates need to be found. It is wise to find more than one sponsor during one's career otherwise one might end up being promoted to one's sponsor's role but no further, as one of the interviewees pointed out. Finally, a small number of the interviewees talked about the danger of aligning oneself to a falling star, and the potentially negative impact a sponsor's failing career can have on his or her protégée's career. It is not enough to find a good sponsor early on and then always rely on him or her for access and visibility in the right circles. Sponsorship is a dynamic process. A woman needs to be aware of how power changes at the top of an organization, and has to find new advocates as her career takes her in new directions. A senior manager in the finance industry pointed out:

> I have worked with very good and very supportive people and with people who trusted me, which has allowed me to develop. I have

also developed personal relationships with key decision-makers who have an effect on my career. I have been able to accurately gauge who the most important people for my career are, which has been important for me. (Senior manager, finance industry)

Building a reputation

Building a reputation for the reliable delivery of results is an important prerequisite for working at senior management level. It helps a woman to gain cooperation and buy in to her ideas.

Without this early exposure to challenging assignments I would not have achieved my current role as quickly. I progressed quickly from a graduate position and was promoted two or three times within the organization. Through this role I could demonstrate my ability. It was a job well done. I had to outperform peers and demonstrate that I can survive and thrive in a competitive environment. I also demonstrated loyalty and hard work. I worked long hours early on in my career. (Emma Cariaga, Head of Strategic Projects, Land Securities Group)

The consulting experience overall has opened doors for me. My first boss was ex-[name of consultancy firm] too ... I could relate better to him as I knew how he works and thinks. Also ex-consultants hire ex-consultants. This experience has given others a benchmark. They say 'If she did this, she will be able to do XYZ.' It has given me a brand name. (Middle manager, FTSE 100 company)

The reputation a woman has acquired during an early stretch assignment lays the foundations for future career success but she will have to continue to work hard to maintain and further solidify her track record and reputation as her career progresses.

SUPPORT

Support is important for each of the critical job assignments described in this book. However, it may be particularly important for this first assignment. All the accounts of the early stretch assignments the interviewees talked about had positive outcomes. While they were utterly challenging, the outcome was ultimately a positive one, the interviewees took away learning and self-confidence, and the assignment was a real career booster. Had these assignments been less successful, which could easily have been the case, then the short- and medium-term outcomes might have been different. A number of the interviewees talked about adversity during their careers – being made redundant, in some cases more than once, leaving organizations because of personal conflicts with their bosses, or failing projects. Every interviewee was very honest about how these situations had become temporary setbacks for them, both in terms of their personal confidence and their career progression. For the majority of these women, though, these setbacks occurred after they had already achieved career success that they could look back over and build on to regain their confidence. If an early stretch assignment ends negatively, the impact may be greater and it may take a woman longer to regain her confidence before she is ready to take on another challenge. There is little or no track record of success at this early stage in a woman's career for her to fall back on, therefore a manager's support is particularly important. Early stretch assignments work best if they are stretching but not overwhelming. A manager's role in understanding where the stretch stops and where the overload starts is important. While stretch assignments are important because they take a person out of his or her comfort zone, a woman needs to have a realistic chance of succeeding.[7] Managers provided several different forms of support. A number of the interviewees, for example, talked about receiving feedback from their managers. DeRue and Wellman found that receiving feedback allowed a person to deal with higher levels of developmental pressure before experiencing the detrimental effects of being overwhelmed by a challenge.[8] One interviewee described the ideal combination of manager support during an early stretch assignment as a manager who allows a woman space to work out problems while still being able to meet regularly to talk through issues. A senior manager made an equally important point when she pointed out how her manager had made it safe for her to fail. Furthermore, managers also play an important part in helping a woman to access resources and open doors, which ensures that she has a realistic chance of succeeding in her early stretch assignment.

TIMING

With this first critical job assignment, the ideal timing is in the title – early. The earlier the first stretch assignment takes place, the better.

It provides an accelerated introduction to organizational life and its challenges, and helps to put young women on the high-potential radar and equip them with a sponsor who can open doors for them. Learning to work with senior managers early in one's career provides a great long-term advantage, as does getting into the habit of taking calculated risks and learning from some of the failures associated with them.

SUMMARY

An early stretch assignment puts a woman on the fast track, and by gaining sponsorship it allows her to skip a few steps in her early career. This in turn may help a woman make the difficult transition from middle to senior management before she has to make a decision about whether to have children or not, as we saw in Chapter 3. Early stretch assignments put women in situations that are far beyond their level of experience and are a trial by fire. A woman has to learn how to be confident while out of her depth, discover how to build credibility and work with senior stakeholders, and all this at the same time as learning about organizational life and herself in this new environment. Women come away from this assignment strengthened in the knowledge that they can do the apparently impossible if they try hard enough, and develop their personal strengths. Their confidence is vastly increased and they take away the all-important prize of emotional intelligence. Early stretch assignments also provide lessons in, and an appetite for, risk-taking. Women gain career benefits by building a reputation as a deliverer of excellent work and as a result acquire senior sponsorship, a key ingredient for their ongoing career success. A manager's support during this early challenge is important, as this learning opportunity can quickly turn into an overwhelming experience that may make the woman reluctant to take on new challenges in the near future. As the title of this chapter suggests, the earlier this type of assignment takes place, the better.

TAKING ACTION

- **Are you in the right place?** Is your manager known for offering his or her team opportunities to show what they can really do? Or are the people around you risk-averse and not interested in helping you to develop? Is this likely to change in the future? If not, look around the organization to locate managers who regularly offer their teams stretch assignments.
- **Make the most of what you have.** If your current role does not stretch you enough, what else can you take on that is valued by the organization and is therefore likely to attract attention? Can you broaden the scope of the project? Can you add extra deliverables that senior managers will value? Taking on additional responsibility and working harder for the sake of it will, however, not achieve much; consider carefully what types of challenges will stretch you and at the same time add value in the eyes of the senior managers around you. Talk to your manager. The key objective is to find opportunities to operate outside your comfort zone and to gain senior management visibility.
- **In the depth of it already.** If you are already dealing with a challenging assignment, consider whether you have enough support to give you a realistic opportunity of succeeding. If not, talk to your manager about the need for additional resources. Asking for support is not about throwing your hands up and saying, 'I cannot do this'; it is about assessing realistically whether you can remove a road block on your own, or not, after you have already tried a number of different approaches. Allowing a project to derail because you did not ask for assistance early enough will not gain you the sponsorship you are seeking. Knowing when to draw on a manager's support to help remove road blocks and ensure the continued success of a project is a valued skill.

5

INTERNATIONAL ASSIGNMENTS AND GLOBAL ROLES: WORKING ABROAD

Abroad you have to try something new as your usual approach is unlikely to work.

(Jenny Newton, Senior Manager, Information Technology and Services Industry)

As businesses become more global, international experience is increasingly valuable. You need to have immersed yourself in it and 'touched it, felt it and lived it'.

(Senior Manager, FTSE 100 Company)

Nothing prepares a leader for running a global organization quite as well as having spent some time abroad to personally experience the difficulties of executing projects and delivering results in a different culture. As we saw in Chapter 1, the lack of international experience has been mentioned as a reason for women not progressing to senior roles.

This chapter explores two different types of international experience. First, the classic international assignment or overseas posting, where a manager is sent abroad for a few months or even years to run local operations, set up a new business unit or work on a special project. Second, it explores global roles, where a manager remains in her home country but is responsible for one or more international regions. Frequent travel is a requirement of this type of international experience. Both types of international experience bring their unique difficulties, but they also have a number of challenges in common, such as building credibility with local teams and customers, and delivering in other cultures. With increasing globalization, the need for international assignments and global roles is steadily increasing.

International experience is not only important for individual managers as preparation for senior management roles; organizations also need to be able to deploy people successfully abroad in order to move expertise around the globe and to compete effectively in the global economy.[1]

The area that has traditionally received more research attention is the international assignment, which involves the complete relocation of a manager abroad. However, similar to the glass ceiling that keeps women from moving beyond a certain level of seniority in an organization, statistics point to what has been called a 'glass border' – the difficulty for women of obtaining an international assignment. The total number of women on international assignments is still relatively low and the numbers, not surprisingly, depend on the industry sector, ranging from 6 percent in construction and engineering to about 30 percent in the non-profit sector, with an average of 15 percent across sectors.[2,3] Women chosen for international assignments seem to have a different profile from their male counterparts. There is evidence that, while men are sent abroad on international assignments at middle and senior management level, often being married and with children, women tend to be younger, in a narrower range of professions, generally single and, not surprisingly, have more junior roles.[4] Furthermore, of those women who take on international assignments, fewer seem to be entrusted with major projects.[5] They also tend to be placed in countries where their gender is unlikely to cause a problem in getting work done.[6]

Global roles have received less research attention, but with advances in technology they are on the increase and are replacing some traditional international assignments. As part of their global roles, managers frequently travel abroad for days or weeks at a time. This type of international experience brings its own challenges, as the following quote from a senior manager shows: 'I had no social life ... it was an intense time but I loved the kick. These are some of my best memories. I [travelled regularly] to Egypt, Romania and Central Africa' (Senior Manager, FTSE 100 company).

Not surprisingly, international experience is seen as one of the most formative experiences as it takes a woman out of her comfort zone in so many different ways. It provides a broad range of experiences and is seen as a great way of increasing a manager's ability to deal with project challenges and people issues.[7] One senior manager reported that it was a complete shock to the system and as such provided real learning. She felt that the further she was from her comfort zone, the more she learned.

Working internationally, either in the form of a classic international assignment, or in a global role with significant travel commitments, was the third most frequently mentioned type of job assignment during the interviews (after working in a different environment and creating something new). Also, where an assignment was classed as falling predominantly into one of the other major categories, such as creating something new (see Chapter 9) or dealing with problems and crises (see Chapter 11), a number of these assignments often also entailed a significant international element. The global role was mentioned somewhat more frequently than the international assignment.

JOB-SPECIFIC CHALLENGES

The challenges for women on international assignments are manifold. Many women who go abroad on international assignments describe their working lives at home as safe, with a trusted network of colleagues and allies, an understanding of what is expected, and an established track record and successful performance to date. Once abroad, it is not just the job that is new but the context too. The new role brings with it new markets and customers, new legislation and working practices, and new organizational structures and politics, to name just a few. And the lack of support networks also serves to make an international assignment challenging.

Getting the job

This first challenge is particularly prominent for international assignments, and while the interviewees rarely mentioned it, it is a well-recognized problem in the existing literature on this topic. Therefore, I want to draw attention briefly to this point. While women are sometimes seen as being more suitable for international assignments because of their strong interpersonal skills, which help them to build new relationships and deal with cultural differences, they nevertheless seem to fall at the first hurdle and find it difficult to obtain international assignments.[8] One of the main reasons women are less likely to be chosen for international assignments is because of stereotypical thinking and assumptions about women working abroad. Single women away from home are regarded as more vulnerable to harassment, while married women cause concern because of antici-pated family and dual-career tensions.[9] The challenges of accommo-dating dual-career couples on international assignments are regarded as being almost insurmountable. As we saw in Chapter 3, women have to ask, often repeatedly, to obtain the roles they want and this holds particularly true if the desired role is an international assignment. Women have to fight the perception that they are either not ready or not interested in international assignments. Women may, however, also be holding themselves back and may underrate their readiness for international assignments. Connerley and colleagues found that while men and women were rated by their supervisors as performing equally well in their jobs, women were rated as significantly less ready for international assignments than their male colleagues.[10] Interest-ingly, women rated themselves as being less ready for international assignments than did their male colleagues, and less ready than rated by their supervisors. Given the challenges of a trailing spouse, and in particular trailing children, women might genuinely feel less ready to move abroad than their male colleagues. Finding the right time to take on an international assignment is critical, as we will see later in this chapter.

Out there on your own

Again, this challenge refers mainly to international assignments. It involves staying abroad on your own without a partner or a social network of friends, and often also being the only person from the organization in situ, with little vital support from head office. The fol-lowing comments illustrate these points well:

> I stayed abroad for four to six months and lived in an apartment on my own which is a lonely experience. I had to have extra confidence and resilience as it was not just challenging to do the project work but also to stay abroad for a long period of time. (Anja Madsen, Operations Development Manager, Tesco)

> [You have to take on] a lot of responsibility as you are there on your own. I was in Slovenia during the time of the Balkan war. Later I spent one year in Hungary and was here during the time of the collapse of the Soviet bloc. I was working on banking projects and it was very male-dominated. I had to operate in a different

culture without a support network. (Cathryn Riley, UK Commercial Director, Aviva)

This lack of support is often felt strongly, and the experience of isolation for women on international assignments has been reported elsewhere.[11] Just as women in their home country often do not have role models, mentors and easy access to senior networks, women on international assignments report similar experiences, which further add to their feelings of isolation.[12]

Being on the outside

Feeling like an outsider is experienced both by women on international assignments and those in global roles, and can be caused by a number of different factors. A lack of knowledge, for example, of local customs or the local language can make inclusion more difficult initially. One interviewee also talked about being sent on an international assignment for only a few months which meant that the local team did not make any attempt to integrate her. She was not going to be there for long enough for the local team to regard it as worth their while to make the effort to do so. Another interviewee talked about how her integration into the new team was threatened when the boss who had brought her into the team moved on and she was left without local support and sponsorship, which hampered her integration. Without integration into the local team, it is difficult, if not impossible, for the new expatriate manager to deliver results.

I was in a different country and seen as an outsider. It takes time to develop relationships. I was there for a limited amount of time only and therefore the local team did not count on me for the long-term and didn't engage with me. Also, the position of the person who had hired me was unstable and he moved on. As I was there only for a short period of time my role wasn't restructured and I was left unsupported. People didn't do what I asked them to do. (Middle manager, FTSE 100 company)

I didn't know the industry very well and worked from outside the organization. I was seen as an outsider. I created strategic recommendations for operations but the operators were sceptical as to how feasible these recommendations were. I tried to mitigate this by getting someone from the organization into the working group. Then there was the language barrier ... the project was in Poland. I also felt quite young ... I was talking to senior executives at the age of 23 in a country where I didn't speak the language. I had to deal with preconceptions about what I could add. To deal with this situation, I tried to learn as much as possible from my manager. I overcompensated by working long hours ... I was an insecure overachiever. I had to deal with huge issues in a three-month time-frame. I solved them but I didn't have much support from the company. (Anja Madsen, Operations Development Manager, Tesco)

My tried and tested approaches don't work here

In addition to integrating into the new team and being regarded as someone who adds value, the interviewees talked about having to get used to a different way of working. New skills and qualities are required, and results are achieved differently than they are back home. This challenge was reported in connection with both international assignments and global roles. Interviewees recalled:

I encountered new ways of working ... my director was ex-[name of consultancy firm] and had a very established management consulting approach to work. He always expected a one-page Power-Point presentation at every meeting with him. Initially I felt that my point of view was not valuable and very different from that of the rest of the team. (Middle manager, FTSE 100 company)

The European division was dysfunctional. There were lots of [people of one European nationality] and a different way of working ... it was very fluid and not decisive enough. I had to think about how to make an impact and ... a difference. It was political due to this clique and it was a very male-oriented, macho environment (Senior manager, FTSE 100 company)

I have worked in lots of different countries and have started up new businesses there. I had to be aware of differences and ensure that I don't use a cookie-cutter approach. (Catherine May, Group Director of Corporate Affairs, Centrica)

Leading global virtual teams

This challenge applies mainly to women who are in global roles and have responsibility for globally-dispersed teams which they lead from the home office:

> I was in an international role ... and I needed to work differently because of the international angle. I had to work remotely with the team and then work intensely with the local teams while I was there. I had to make sure that people got the message and wouldn't go local again once I had left. You have to make sure you don't have an argument while you are there and that you do not leave on bad terms. Have the argument before you go there and then sort it out so you can leave on good terms. I learned how to influence the agenda remotely and how to pick the right teams locally. (Orlagh Hunt, Group Human Resources Director, RSA Group)

The challenges of managing teams remotely are well recognized. Building trust and a sense of team identity in the absence of physical proximity, monitoring performance at a distance and understanding how much virtual interaction each team member needs are some of the challenges that are often cited.[13]

Coming home

This challenge is encountered exclusively by women on international assignments, particularly when abroad for longer periods of time. Interestingly, the interviewees in this study again did not actively refer to this difficulty, but as it is prominent in the research literature I will briefly outline the challenges associated with repatriation. Once back home, a significant percentage of repatriates leave their employers within 12–18 months of returning.[14] It is often difficult to fulfill the expectations of returning expatriates for career advancement at the home office, particularly when a manager has been away for a long time.[15] New skills are often not used on the return to base, and companies increasingly refuse to guarantee expats a position on their return, as they expect the home operations to shrink and international operations to grow. Problems with repatriation are particularly likely in organizations where there is no explicit policy regarding international assignments, and where repatriates have to find their own opportunities. Not all global organizations are truly global, and where international assignments are not actively encouraged, managed and supported, the danger of derailment is significantly higher.[16]

WOMEN-SPECIFIC CHALLENGES

Working in patriarchal societies

As we saw earlier in this chapter, the main women-specific challenges for women abroad are working in patriarchal societies and dealing with childcare arrangements and trailing spouses. Many of the interviewees referred to the macho, male-dominated working style and attitude toward women while working abroad. Interestingly, however, there is also evidence that women abroad are often given 'foreigner' status, which protects them from some of the discriminatory behaviors experienced by local women.[17] In a small study of female expatriates from Western multinational corporations who had been posted to Taiwan, Tzeng, for example, found that Caucasian women were treated favourably by Taiwanese colleagues because of their 'foreigner' status.[18] However, it was reported that gender stereotypes were still expressed by their Caucasian male colleagues. Interestingly, American-Chinese women were treated according to local norms for Taiwanese women and experienced sexism and other barriers. This experience was also described by one of the interviewees, who used to travel abroad regularly as part of one of her global roles: 'I was a white woman coming from a different country. I had more respect as I came from headquarters. The playing field was levelled for me. I also had the CEO's support and I was seen as an expert' (Senior manager, FTSE 100 company).

Transnational couples and trailing families

In addition to the difficulties already examined, married women with children experience significant family-related challenges while on international assignments. Linehan and Walsh found that a lack of emotional and domestic support is frequently reported by these women, as they have left behind support networks and trusted childcare arrangements. Furthermore, managing the relationship with a trailing spouse, who may have given up his job back home with no role to go to in the new host country, causes additional concerns for many of these women. Managers whose families relocated for an international assignment noted that organizing family life was more difficult than the job itself. For those women who had not relocated families abroad but who lived as split households, some felt that personal relationships had suffered because of the demands of balancing career and home life, particularly when spending long periods away from home.[19]

A small number of the interviewees worked in global roles with significant travel requirements while pregnant or while having very young children to care for, which led to unhelpful remarks and attitudes, as one interviewee recalled:

> I became pregnant while I was in an international role. People were intending to be helpful but made remarks like: 'You won't want this level of role when you have a child.' But they forgot that I am the breadwinner. The mortgage won't get paid if I don't work. When I came back from maternity leave I did all the international trips I had to do. In the first year after I had my child I felt that I had to prove to others that I can do it all. (Senior manager, FTSE 100 company)

IN FOCUS: A VILLAGE OF SUPPORT

Combining a demanding senior executive career with being a mother requires an extensive support network. In these situations, women have to rely on a 'village of support', a concept introduced in Chapter 2. The two main functions provided by a woman's support network outside of work are, first, practical help with childcare, and second, emotional support and encouragement.

Childcare

The vast majority of the interviewees work full-time and their children's care is provided by trusted nannies, a nursery or school. The after-school care is provided either by au pairs, grandparents or partners who work flexibly. As well as this there are the 'extras' such as organizing all this care and making sure there is emergency cover in case a nanny or au pair is ill, or dropping a child off at

---

nursery in the morning and picking him/her up in the evening. Of the interviewees with children, 39 percent stated that these extra responsibilities are shared equally with their partner. In 15 percent and 14 percent of the cases, respectively, the extra childcare is again shared, but the woman or her partner take on a bit more. In 14 percent, the woman's partner is the main carer, and 7 percent stated that the extras are covered by grandparents; 11 percent stated that the extra childcare is taken on entirely by the woman.

Let us take a look at the type of help that partners provide with childcare: 'My husband is very supportive. He will always help and pick up the children. He also travels a lot so there is a lot of juggling. He accepts that I have to work away from home and that my days are long' (Senior manager, FTSE 100 company).

A number of partners make a linear, male-like career progression possible for the woman by putting their career in second place and working flexibly, part-time or not at all in order to take care of the couple's children and to manage the home. This means that the breadwinner role largely falls to the woman: 'My husband is the main carer. He is self-employed and works two days a week. We have a nanny for those two days' (Senior manager, FTSE 100 company); 'I have had a lot of support from my husband. He deliberately gave up his job so that I could do my job. I never had to worry about home life' (Senior manager, FTSE 100 company).

Parents were mentioned on a number of occasions as providing much-needed additional support with childcare, either on an ongoing basis or during holiday time or particularly demanding times at work:

My parents have always been there as another pillar. The children have an amazing relationship with their grandparents and it is still family if the grandparents look after the children. My mum cooks tea for them, cares for them when they are ill and takes them out during school holidays. My father is at the house if a job needs to be done. We pay my parents for their time. (Senior manager, FTSE 100 company)

If I cannot get home on time there is always my mum. She was a grandmother in waiting and is very keen to get involved with her grandchildren. (Senior manager, FTSE 100 company)

69

Emotional support and encouragement

Where women have partners, their support is key to helping the women to fulfill their potential. A partner gives a woman confidence that she can do it, that she is ready for the next move and that she should 'just go for it'. Being able to listen, being a sounding board and discussing work-related concerns are other important types of support that partners provide. Many women with children talked about the recognition their partners had for their careers:

My husband never had any issues with me working. When I was unsure about whether I could go back after our second child was born he said to me, are you sure you won't regret this later on? (Senior manager, FTSE 100 company)

Throughout my career my husband has provided support. He has the ability to listen and to discuss issues. (Senior manager, FTSE 100 company)

The other source of emotional support that was mentioned by a number of the women were other women at similar levels of seniority as themselves, as well as sisters and other female friends, who act as a sounding board and a confidante:

I have a close female friend in a senior management position who is my confidante. (Senior manager, FTSE 100 company)

My sisters have been important. They have the ability to listen and discuss issues. They have affection for me and are role models for me. They are professional women, too. (Senior manager, FTSE 100 company)

LESSONS LEARNED

The challenges posed by global roles and international assignments are clearly significant, but so is the learning gained from these experiences. A highly effective time for personal development is a time when a person comes face-to-face with his or her own assumptions about who they are and how the world works. The ensuing questioning and realigning of thought patterns and strongly held beliefs bring about effective development. Living and working in a new country, ideally even on a new continent, provides such conditions for profound learning.[20] Learning about the importance of relationships, thinking and acting globally while at the same time considering the local context, and, in Wilson and Dalton's words, 'seeing situations through the eyes of others, effective expats are often humbled by profound learning about themselves and their culture' (p. 32).[21] Furthermore, for many women, going abroad offers new opportunities to gain leadership skills, as roles are often more senior, even if they are set in strategically less important business units. As part of this move to more senior roles, some women have learned important lessons about making decisions and commanding respect.

Flexibility and adaptability

The most frequently mentioned lesson from working abroad or working in a global role was an increased adaptability and flexibility of approach. To be successful in a foreign context requires an open mind and a flexible approach. This flexibility is developed through working with people in the new host country, dealing with local issues and operating in a new legislative and regulatory environment. Many of the interviewees talked about learning that there is more than one way of doing things. This type of learning is difficult to achieve without leaving the home country:

> We got to meet people from all over the world. Travelling around the world makes you aware of who you are as a person. All countries are very different: cultures, references and needs. And the trade of a salesman is to understand that not everything comes in the same size. (Sophie Turner Laing, Managing Director, Entertainment and News, British Sky Broadcasting)

> It has helped me develop cultural awareness, which is important because it helps you to understand what others want and why other types of delivery are important in different situations. For example, US companies want short-term quarterly results, whereas French companies are longer-term-focused and they value the elegance and academic brilliance of a solution. I learned that there are multiple routes to getting to the end – not just one way. Without this experience I would have had only one style. (Jenny Newton, Senior Manager, Information Technology and Services Industry)

71

Working abroad forced me to challenge my own assumptions about how results are best achieved. It was tempting to rely on what had worked well for me in the past but I soon realised that I would not be able to achieve the same outcomes. I had to make the time to find locally acceptable ways of getting to results. It was frustrating but it has made me much more flexible. (Senior manager, FTSE 100 company)

Resilience

As we saw at the start of this chapter, working in a global role, and particularly working abroad on an international assignment, not only bring job-related challenges but also challenges outside of work. As such, home life does not initially provide respite from the struggles a woman may face in her new role; instead it adds to them. Trying to sort out accommodation, childcare and dealing with the concerns of a trailing spouse, all add to a woman's difficulties. It is not surprising that international experience tests a woman's resilience.

One senior manager talked about the experience of frequent global travel being a lonely experience and that she had not always been treated well. She had toughened up as a result of this.

CAREER BENEFITS

A big fish in a small pond

International assignments are often seen as a prerequisite for moving to senior management positions. And in organizations where they are not seen as a prerequisite, they nevertheless help women to differentiate themselves from the rest. They provide that little bit extra that helps a woman to stand out. The HR director of a FTSE100 company put the developmental nature of an international assignment down to the additional leadership responsibilities that can often be obtained while abroad:

International assignments are increasingly important, as companies are becoming more global now. People have more autonomy abroad and more opportunities to be the CEO than at head office. You can do your own thing. People often enjoy it and it provides exposure and visibility. (HR director, FTSE 100 company)

Some of the interviewees talked about the 'big fish in a small pond' experience. Operations abroad are often smaller, which means that the woman can take a more prominent role. The smaller size of the operation also allowed the interviewees to be in charge of taking decisions, and to see the impact of their decisions straight away. While they may previously have only contributed to decisions at head office, once abroad they are responsible for making important decisions themselves. Their time abroad helped them to learn to make decisions on the go, work with the best available data, trust their instincts and realize that they enjoy the responsibility that comes with making your own decisions. In addition to the decision-making, the interviewees also learned about other aspects of working as a leader, such as honing their people management skills and building a power base, as the following comments show:

> This experience helped me to learn how easy it is to make assumptions. I felt disempowered in this situation at my [senior] level, which made me think about how people further down in the organization must feel. It made me think more about the impact of changes in the organization, and how to truly reach and engage people. It helped me hone my leadership skills. (Cathryn Riley, UK Commercial Director, Aviva)

> I realized half way through my six-month assignment that I should have built my power base better. People were competing for power and the way you perform in the first month sets expectations for the remainder of the time. I learned about having to set firmer structures earlier on. You need to let people know that you are in charge and follow through if they are not delivering for you. (Middle manager, FTSE 100 company)

Understanding international business

Working internationally significantly increases a woman's international business acumen, as she has 'touched it, felt it and lived it'. And this international business acumen is a much valued attribute in a global world:

> It gave me exposure to a global organization and diverse cultures. I learned to deal with the head office in the US and gained insights into global head office considerations versus regional

considerations. I learned how to manage myself in a global arena. (Senior manager, FTSE 100 company)

I went to Singapore for 18 months and set up my own food broker-age service. This allowed me to look at the UK through interna-tional eyes ... Afterwards I joined an international organization and ran their European business for five years. Then I ran it globally. I moved it from low to high returns. I built and managed a fan-tastic team across 25 markets. It gave me top-notch general man-agement experience and I developed an understanding of working internationally. (Senior manager, finance industry)

In addition to increased international business acumen, the inter-viewees also talked about gaining other types of experience that were valued back home, such as operational experience and the ability to create something from nothing.

SUPPORT

A significant amount of information is available about the type of organ-izational support that helps expatriates to deal effectively with the chal-lenges associated with living and working abroad. However, the majority of the interviewees reported receiving relatively little support from their organizations, and this is very much in line with findings in other stud-ies, as many organizations send their managers abroad ill-equipped.[22] Let us look briefly at what types of support have been found to be helpful.

First, incorporating a readiness assessment as part of a yearly performance appraisal ensures that women are not excluded from in-ternational assignment opportunities. While an international assign-ment may not be practical for a woman at a particular time because of her family's circumstances, this situation may change a few years down the line and the woman may then be ready to take on an assignment abroad. Furthermore, overcoming stereotypes back at the home office is important.[23] Organizations are advised not to assume that women do not want to be posted on international assignments, or that women abroad may not fare well. Female managers should also not be confused with female spouses, who are often the reason for men leaving their in-ternational assignments prematurely.[24] Evidence suggests that women managers are often very successful while on an international assign-ment.[25] Once a woman has agreed to an international assignment, there are a number of very practical, highly beneficial things with which an organization can provide support, such as language, customs and etiquette training. All of these provide an important foundation to help with integration and building relationships once abroad. Despite its proven effectiveness, this type of training does not routinely take place, and when it does, spouses and children are seldom included.[26] Women in particular benefit from training that is designed specifically to meet their needs; for example, behavioral coping strategies for working in patriarchal societies, and protocol and dress codes.[27]

With the demand for international assignments forecast to rise, it is unlikely that single men and women will be able to satisfy all the demand. Therefore, organizations need to look more closely at the challenges of trailing partners and providing career opportunities for them too.[28] Another factor that helps women with families to relocate is an adequate lead time to help in relocating the entire family. To help trailing families adjust as quickly as possible, organizations can help by providing information about desirable neighborhoods, housing costs, schools, medical facilities, transportation and childcare. To ensure the expatriate manager's success in her role, setting clear business goals, providing access to networks of successful former expatriates, and a mentor who helps the woman keep in touch with her home country, are all helpful. Finally, repatriation to the home country has to be carefully planned some time in advance to ensure that a challenging role recognizing the woman's development and increased capability after the international assignment is available for her back in her home country.[29]

In addition to organizational support, personal support networks are important for women while working in global roles with frequent travel, or while on international assignments. Because of the additional burden caused by travel or by having to set up a new life abroad, the support of husbands, children and even nannies and maids is essential during this time.[30]

TIMING

Sending single men and women abroad clearly reduces one of the significant sources of difficulties, as trailing spouses or families are less likely to be an issue. A woman's current life stage influences her attitude toward international assignments, and women without children, or those with older children at boarding school or university, find such assignments more acceptable. Single female expatriates or those with young children express concerns about whether they would accept a (further) international assignment because of childcare issues:[31]

> It is important as it gives you a different perspective on life and work … it needs to be at least 12–18 months. Do it early on, as it is easier to [fit into] your personal life … it is expensive for organizations to relocate people and entire families. (Anna Capitanio, Vice-President, Organizational Effectiveness and M&A HR, BT Global Services)

Early postings abroad also seem to help managers to learn important lessons and avoid costly mistakes later at senior management level. The sooner foreign elements are introduced to a manager's work, the greater the chances are that the manager will be effective in today's global world.[32] This is echoed in the following comment:

> If you do international assignments at a junior level then you get international exposure which is OK but you don't get senior CEO-type exposure. Therefore you may have to do international assignments multiple times. (HR Director, FTSE100 company)

SUMMARY

Working in an international context brings many challenges, such as being on your own and being an outsider, having to find new ways of working, and leading virtual teams. Women-specific challenges of working in patriarchal societies and dealing with childcare arrangements are additional trials. However, working abroad also provides a woman with many important lessons for personal development. Flexibility and adaptability, and the resilience to deal with both work and home challenges are important skills learned. Organizations value international assignments and global roles as they provide international business acumen, which is crucial for organizations to operate effectively in a global market. It also helps promising managers to try their hand at senior roles in smaller organizations, and gain experience of senior-level decision-making.

Organizations can help in many practical ways to increase the likelihood of success, such as ongoing readiness assessment, and language and cultural training. However, many organizations provide little help. Going abroad while a woman is still single and childless is the easiest time for her to go, and it is the most convenient also for her organization.

Another good time for women to take on an international assignment is when her children are older and may not have to be relocated as they are at boarding school or university. To ensure that women are integrated into the local organization, roles should be at least 12–18 months long.

TAKING ACTION

- **Readiness assessment.** Are you ready for an international assignment or global role? Do your own readiness assessment. Where are you in life, and who do you have to include in your readiness assessment? Your partner also needs to be included in your readiness assessment. Discuss your desire to work abroad or in a global role with everyone in your family who may be affected. Planning early is key, and being able to demonstrate to your manager that you (and, if applicable, your partner and family) are ready for a global role or an international assignment will increase your chances of securing such a role.

- **Organizational support.** Does your organization have an official international assignment policy? How well are managers supported when they go abroad, and how valued is the experience they acquire there? Does the organization provide access to former expatriates and local networks? What other practical support is provided? Make a list of the support that is most important for you and talk to your manager and HR team about how you can get this support.

- **The value of international assignments.** Have you seen other managers in your organization return successfully from international assignments? Are their skills valued, and has the experience allowed them to progress faster in the organization? Or have most of the managers left the organization shortly after their return because of a lack of career progression? Talk to colleagues who have returned from international assignments to learn about their experiences of coming back home.

- **Alternatives.** If now is not the right time for an international assignment or a global role, what other options are there for you to gain international experience that will put you into a better position to get an international assignment or global role once the time is right? Consider working on projects where you are part of a virtual global team, or consider short-term projects that may involve one or two business trips abroad.

6

OPERATIONAL EXPERIENCE:
THE DAY-TO-DAY RUNNING OF A BUSINESS
AND P&L ACCOUNTABILITY

*If you have an appetite for senior roles you need to have the experience
of running a business. In line roles you don't get P&L experience and
project management is not a substitute.*
> (Anna Capitanio, Vice-President, Organizational
> Effectiveness and M&A HR, BT Global Services)

*There will be times when the numbers don't come in and you need
to have the guts to ride it out. It's not pleasant but you have to
persevere.*
> (Mary Lawrance, Founder of Cariance Executive Search)

Operational experience is a key stepping stone on the way to the
top position in any organization. It provides a woman with a vital
understanding of the day-to-day running of a business. In these
roles, women are responsible for operating and improving the systems that produce and deliver an organization's products or services.
Manufacturing, purchasing, supply chain management, distribution
and call centre operations are all examples of operational roles (also
often referred to as line roles or front-line roles), and there are many
more. Which roles are classed as operational depends on the products a company is producing, or the services it is offering. However,
operational roles are always at the core of what a company delivers, as opposed to functional roles which provide support services
such as human resources (HR), legal and finance. While no modern
organization could function without these support functions, they
are not deemed to be central to a company's day-to-day operation.
Without operational experience, aspiring to the CEO role is unlikely

to be a realistic target unless you are progressing in finance, one of the few exceptions, as chief finance officers (CFOs) are deemed to be credible contenders for CEO roles while no other functional heads are. As we saw in Chapter 3, however, most women still progress in functional roles such as HR, legal, finance or marketing, and do not tend to have substantial amounts of operational experience. They are even less likely to progress in the operational area to general management roles with profit and loss (P&L) accountability. The lack of operational experience is cited repeatedly as a reason as to why so few women are seen in top jobs.[1,2]

What makes operational experience so important for career progression? There are a number of contenders, such as managing large numbers of people, dealing with crises and learning to juggle opposing business demands, but the one thing that has been mentioned time and again is P&L accountability. True P&L accountability is only held by a very small number of people at senior level in general management roles, who are responsible for both the revenue generating and cost producing parts of the business, such as sales, and the day-to-day operations of a business. At a less senior level, operational experience does, however, mean working in a very clearly output-focused environment where operations or sales numbers are reported on a weekly, if not daily, basis. This output-focused, measureable way of working provides an acute understanding of costs, margins and efficiencies, and as such a clear understanding of the core drivers of business. A senior executive with a general management background illustrates the importance of understanding the value of money in the following comment:

> Even in government you have to make value judgments. You should get this experience from the beginning. You should care about resource allocation and you need to be sensitive to it. Cost-saving is a part of it and it has to be your way of life when thinking about value. You need to learn to see the value of money. You need to think carefully about any investment, even in boom times. I need to stress how important it is to get this experience early on. (Senior manager, FTSE 100 company)

While senior executives in functional roles rarely have exposure to P&L experience, they also emphasize the importance of being financially literate, as the following comment shows: 'I have no direct P&L responsibility but you need to have competence in this area. Most people in big business don't get P&L accountability but you need to be financially literate' (Senior manager, FTSE 100 company).

With increasing seniority, women start to run parts of a business and become business managers with responsibility for the many different elements of the company they are running. Charan and colleagues report that many of the male and female senior executives they have worked with state that this challenge is a most enjoyable one as it provides executives with the opportunity to be in charge of both making and selling the company's products or services.[3] As part of this role, they have full P&L accountability. This point is echoed by a senior manager who is currently heading up a functional area but who also has a strong operational background.

> The best way to get commercial experience is to run a business. It gives you P&L responsibility, responsibility for people, responsibility for goods and services, responsibility for it all. Women who are running operations and therefore large teams are better at it due to their emotional intelligence. (Senior manager, FTSE 100 company)

JOB-SPECIFIC CHALLENGES

Charan and his colleagues list a number of challenges for leaders who run a business, including being highly visible both inside and outside the organization, receiving a lot less guidance from their immediate bosses, having to deal with great complexity, having to learn to value all the organization's functions to the same extent, and going through a significant shift in thinking style and problem-solving. Charan and his colleagues talk about 'an avalanche of accountability' (p. 85), which few managers are prepared for. They list a set of over 100 different elements that business managers are responsible for, starting from advertising and assets to logos, furnishings and raw materials. We shall come across most of these challenges in the next three sections, when I explore the challenges, lessons learned and career benefits associated with operational experience, and, at a more senior level, with running a business.

Being prepared for visible failure

One of the themes that emerged repeatedly across all the critical job assignments is the importance of delivering and of being perceived as a safe pair of hands to get things done and sort out problems. But there are, of course, times when results are not achieved. These setbacks are not unusual, and the interviewees talked about them in some detail. Operational roles highlight success, or the lack of it, because of output-focused measures that make results easy for everyone to see. Women in operational roles therefore need to have grit and determination in times when expected results are not achieved:

> Lots of women get sucked into corporate roles where they can get very comfortable ... But you need to get back in [to line roles]. A recruiter wants to see the determination to push into front-line roles. You need to steel yourself to get through times when it is difficult to deliver results and have the guts to deal with being sidelined when that happens. Women have the grit and toughness to take front-line roles and often surprise themselves with how well they have done once they have tried it. Do it as early in your career as you can. (Mary Lawrance, Founder of Cariance Executive Search)

> When you are running a P&L you need to be very tough, decisive and have great leadership. If you are not meeting your budget you need to lose people or retrain them or you will have tough conversations with your board. (Alison Carnwath, Chairman, Land Securities Group)

The complexity of running a business

Once a woman reaches the level of business manager roles she has to deal with added complexity. The interviewees talked about looking after larger teams and multiple operational sites, working in more complex matrix set-ups, facing new customers, and running global teams. For many of the interviewees the move to a business management, or managing director, role was a big step up:

> During one career move I felt my new role doubled in scale and quadrupled in complexity from my previous role. I had new customers, a new company and new technology. I did, however, benefit from it sharing some of the characteristics of previous roles. Specifically, it was a highly matrixed organization and some of the senior team had similar ways of working to my previous boss. (Karen Oddey, CEO of an equity-funded specialist electronics company)

When you are running a business you need to show that you can integrate. It is broader than just cross-functional working. You need to think across all the ingredients: business planning, engineering, equipment procurement, advertising. You need business education to do that. You should do it right from the beginning and show that you are curious about the world you work in. (Sheelagh Whittaker, Non-executive Director, Standard Life)

WOMEN-SPECIFIC CHALLENGES

The women-specific challenges of operational experience are formidable and have often been cited as one of the reasons why there are not more women in operational roles.

Long hours, last-minute meetings and unplanned travel

Why is it that women are less likely to have operational experience? The interviewees pointed out that women's emotional intelligence makes them good at managing large teams, and that their problem-solving skills make them good 'fire-fighters'. The following comments outline some of the reasons why we may still only see a small number of women in operational roles and even fewer in general management positions:

> Too few women are running a P&L business. P&L responsibility means you are running the show. Most women, however, wisely think about the implications for their families. It is more demanding on flexibility and time. You need to be available at weekends. Is it worthwhile? But you cannot become a CEO without P&L experience. We need to become better at making those P&L roles more compatible with women's needs. (Anna Capitanio, Vice-President Organizational Effectiveness and M&A, BT Global Services)

> In general management roles the international travel is demanding. Most of our customers are not in the UK. And as all travel is customer-driven it is often unplanned. If customers are US-based, for example, then you have to do late night video calls ... In functional roles the international travel is discretionary and more planned. The head of tax, for example, works on a tax issue with professional

services companies by email and telephone. For the engineer, on the other hand, it is important to solve customer problems and if there are operational problems you have to fly to Bangalore ... You can become a good CFO without too much travel and you can be a top-flight accountant or HR professional under the age of 35. For women, it is easier to work their way up through HR, legal and finance but from there it is also difficult for women to move into general management. (HR director, FTSE 100 company)

Clearly, there are a number of challenges associated with operational roles that make them less attractive to women: the emergency travel, the last-minute, late-night meetings, and the general unplanned nature of the work. Operational responsibility does not allow for a highly planned day or week and as such it is more difficult to combine with family commitments.

IN FOCUS: CHILDREN AND CAREER ADVANCEMENT

This is the most ambitious topic to tackle in a short In Focus section. It is such a wide-ranging and important topic and in many ways at the centre of why women (those with children) are finding it harder to move to senior positions. The interviewees made a number of interesting points I want to share even if these will not address all the aspects of this topic.

The path to senior management roles in large organizations is rocky and windy; not only for women, for men, too. If you want to move to the top, an organization expects commitment. Maximum commitment. All the time. Women, in the same way as men, are prepared to work hard and they are just as good at what they do as their male counterparts. However, when children are added to the equation, this commitment is tested severely. Many quotes illustrate how women with children have to try to maintain as close to the 100 percent commitment as possible, since taking a year off for maternity leave, working part-time or leaving the office at 6pm on the dot every evening are significant career-limiting factors:

I like the Canadian model of shared parental leave to help reduce the amount of time taken by women and to equalize men and women. One year is a long time to be away from work. Things change a lot. Six months off is better. Also, returning part-time is problematic due to the sheer hours of work and the sheer amount of responsibility. There is a huge burden of responsibility at executive level. You have a lot of corporate responsibility. We are now all available 365 days a year. It is also a speed of response issue. But it's a choice – if you can't and don't want to do 16 hours a day then you shouldn't look to go into these senior roles. Gone are the days where the more senior you get the more time you spend on the golf course. (Senior manager, no children)

Organizations that have too much positive discrimination can be detrimental. Far too many women come back part-time and it is difficult to manage a business with lots of part-time people. It is detrimental for a very capable person to take whole years away from work. When you have children you are restricted; you are not at work when they need you. (Senior executive, children)

When you are moving from middle to senior management you need to act like a man professionally. You cannot forget about the company for five months while you have children. You have to give the impression that you are as accessible as the rest of them. If you always leave at 6.30pm that is a problem even if you work long hours by starting early in the morning. You have to be like the men. I haven't seen cases where women are CEOs and they have not done the same hours as the men. Try to be as similar as the others and don't insist that you always have to leave at 6pm. (Senior manager, children)

One senior executive shared her frustration about how long it took her to join the executive committee. She mentioned that she had been operating at the level below the board for many years, and that she has had feedback that she is 'board material'. She speculated during the interview that the reasons it has taken her so long is that she may not have been regarded as being 100 percent committed to the organization because of her childcare responsibilities. When her children were young she used to have to leave at 6pm and when there were meetings in the evening she arrived at the meeting with her bag and coat. Now that her children are older and it does not matter if she comes home half an hour late, she can be more relaxed at evening meetings and stay for the last 20 minutes too. Those interviewees who have had additional support at home, either through a stay-at-home partner or parents who took on caring responsibilities for their grand-children, talked about the benefits of not having to watch the clock in the evening to make sure they left on time.

A number of the most senior interviewees in the sample talked about how they had taken very little maternity leave, how they had stayed in touch with the company while on such leave, and how they had returned to work full-time and continued to work long hours. A number of the senior managers who are operating just below executive committee level, on the other hand, talked about how they had accepted that their careers might temporarily be stalled because they had chosen to take six months of maternity leave rather than six weeks, because they had moved to roles with fewer travel commitments and because they had decided not to look for more senior roles as this would have meant more travel-ling. It must be stressed, though, that these women are still working full-time and in highly demanding roles. They are 'just' not doing the extra little bit that gets them up to the 100 percent commit-ment. These interviewees are clear that this reduction in commit-ment meant a temporary suspension of their career advancement:

> I was responsible for 74 countries and over 10,000 people. Lots of variety, lots of travel. Then I fell pregnant and took six months off. When I returned I was offered the same role again but with a small child I didn't want to do all the travel. I want to put my child to bed at night. I was then offered a role at the same senior level but with a local remit so now I have some flexibility to be at home and pick up my child from daycare. (Senior manager, child)

Some of the interviewees talked about the guilt of not being there for their children. This guilt often seemed to set in when the inter-viewees had to do a lot of travelling, which made it almost impossi-ble to fit work commitments around childcare responsibilities. The flexibility that the interviewee in the previous quote talked about is then completely gone.

In addition to reducing one's commitment, do children reduce the appetite for risk-taking? Three senior managers with children had the following to say:

> Life is so busy. Do you feel secure enough when you have chil-dren [to take risks]? I had my children young. I was not worried.

If this job doesn't work out I can always change my career path. Women are risk-averse. Women's strength is as an enabler but they are not putting their heads above the parapet. (Senior manager, children)

I had had a good career until then but I was ready to take a risk. My children were older and it didn't matter if I would be out of a job if this role wouldn't work out. (Senior manager, children)

My children are getting older. I could do a very big role and want to do it now. (Senior manager, children)

Whether a woman is working at a 95 percent or 100 percent commitment level, combining a senior management career with childcare responsibilities is difficult and a constant juggling act. It also means finding ways of being available for both work and family when each need her. These arrangements leave little or no time for the woman herself.

I am up at 5:30am, clear my inbox and send out a lot of emails. I then go to the gym and make breakfast for the family. I am then at work but between 5.30pm and 7.30pm I am not online. However, I am back online at 8.30pm ... As you get more senior you are afforded more flexibility and have more control over your diary. The roles you take on are more in management and you no longer have to spend an entire week away from the office as you have to in junior roles. There are always trade-offs and you need to be aware of them and understand the full demands of the role. (Senior manager, children)

Can a supportive partner be categorized as a coping strategy for juggling an executive career with family commitments? Maybe not, but he is vital to making the juggling work as he will have to do his share of the childcare:

I had both my children during this time. I went back to work full-time after four months' maternity leave. Three and a half years later I had my second child. There was lots of pressure and lots of juggling. One of us would go in early and come back early and the other would stay for breakfast with the kids and then stay late in the office. We had lots of calls during the day about how to juggle it all. My husband has been a big supporter of my career. I had to work lots of late nights and weekends. (Senior manager, children)

These are exhausting arrangements and for a number of the interviewees there came a time when they had to take a step back or some time out in order to recharge their batteries. These 'time-out' phases never lasted very long, however; one year at the most. The interviewees talked about taking a lower-level role for six months, but would go two steps up again afterwards, or they talked about changing employers in order to work a four-day week only to take on a new role and be responsible for an even bigger area than before.

While being very clear about the opportunity cost of their careers to their families, the interviewees loved their jobs and enjoyed the buzz of a senior management career which gave them the opportunity to make a real difference in their organizations.

LESSONS LEARNED

Getting things done

The interviewees who had moved from a functional to an operational role valued the experience of learning what it takes to implement changes and get things done. This is learning that was reported mainly by the middle managers in the sample who had recently made the transition from functional to operational roles:

This operational experience provided me with high-level project management skills. It helped me to move from [being] a consultant to [being] a consultant who gets things done. I learned how to do things in real life – how decisions impact others in the business, who the right stakeholders are, what the risks of strategic change are, how change can impact the organization positively but also negatively, and what can go wrong. And finally I learned to understand the effort that day-to-day operators need to put into change initiatives in addition to their daily tasks. (Middle manager, FTSE 100 company)

The skills I acquired that were most valued by the organization were being able to develop practical, operational recommendations. (Middle manager, FTSE 100 company)

Making decisions on your own

Learning to make important, far-reaching decisions on your own is probably the most important take-away lesson from senior-level operational experience. In addition to P&L accountability it is a core contributor to building a woman's leadership profile:

> When you are running a business you are the one who makes the final decisions. Women often influence and facilitate decision-making but that is still different to making the actual decisions. It is hard to be on top of the business all the time. (Anna Capitanio, Vice-President Organizational Effectiveness and M&A HR, BT Global Services)

Even if a woman may not yet be in charge of making all the decisions on her own, the benefits of first-hand operational experience to decision-making are clearly felt, as this next comment from a middle manager shows:

> I feel that I need the experience of how to do things and not just of how to help others to do things. It will give me more reassurance when I make decisions ... More operations experience will allow me to make decisions based on more facts and to understand the consequences. It's learning by doing and not observing others. The organization respects operational knowledge more than theoretical knowledge. It will allow me to acquire authority to talk about issues. (Middle manager, FTSE 100 company)

As we saw in the In Focus section in Chapter 4, before women make decisions and take calculated risks they tend to test out their thinking with others first. This is often seen by men as a sign of reluctance to take decisions, as they tend to have a more individualistic decision-making style. Taking the first decision on your own is a key experience for women and one that can trigger a desire for more freedom to make decisions. Once the first important business decision has been taken, the interviewees have often found that they like it and feel more comfortable with it than they thought they would:

> I took responsibility for an additional business unit in the US which was unprofitable. Having reviewed the combined business I decided I needed to exit a line of product developments, and that it would mean downsizing a team. While I had taken downsizing decisions before they had always been part of corporate cost reduction programs. This was the first time I decided to reduce the number of employees in my business unit. I had to get buy-in to the decision from my team and my manager, and then to communicate with the team. I believe telling people they are losing their jobs is one of the hardest roles a general manager has to take. It was a formulative experience for me early in my leadership career. (Senior manager, FTSE 100 company)

CAREER BENEFITS

Having credibility

Gaining credibility is a challenge that the interviewees talked about repeatedly during the interviews, and it emerged as important for a number of different critical job assignments: building credibility as a young woman during an early stretch assignment (see Chapter 4); as a novice after the move to a new industry or function (see Chapter 8); and as an intrapreneur in order to convince others of one's ideas for a new business venture (see Chapter 9). This much-sought-after credibility is something that operational roles and specifically P&L experience give a woman immediately, as the following comments show:

> I gained operations experience from this role, which gave me credibility to talk about operations and I became a more rounded professional. My current boss is from an operational background and is a very practical guy. This experience helped me to get my current role, where I need to understand operational issues. My boss appreciates that I have an operational point of view. (Middle manager, FTSE 100 company)

> Generally you need broad-based skills for senior management roles. You need operational capability and you need to have run something of scale, such as teams, operations or sale. (Senior manager, FTSE 100 company).

A woman is no longer seen as 'only' a functional expert but as having highly valued insights into how the core of the organization works. Just as a degree in a numerate subject, or having worked for a particular consultancy firm, give women a head-start in building credibility in certain situations, so does operational experience. A woman's opinion is taken more seriously straight away and she finds it easier to influence senior managers. One interviewee, who is the head of one of the support functions in her organization, stated how important her operational experience had been in allowing her to be valued as a member of the executive committee. Her direct experience of operational issues makes it very clear to everyone that she can talk knowledgeably about business matters that are outside her functional area.

Visibility

One of the challenges of operational roles is its visibility, particularly at times when results are not achieved. But this visibility is also a strong career booster. When results *are* achieved, they are easy for everyone to see. It makes a woman visible straight away, and puts her at the centre of the organization:

> Women tend to be in HR, are legal counsels, or they are in compliance or accounting, but they are not in sales and P&L roles. Those roles are seen as a necessary overhead but it's difficult to measure output. They make a difference to the organization but not in a visible way. (Senior manager, FTSE 100 company)

And it is not only internal visibility that is increased by operational or P&L roles. Senior operational roles, such as becoming the managing director of a business unit or the CEO of a country operation, also significantly increase a woman's external visibility, as the following comments show: 'This role gave me contacts with businesses and government that I had never had before. I started being known due to press coverage' (Senior manager, finance industry). This next comment refers to a director-level business development role in a financial institution: '[This role] allowed me to get noticed more and to see more people. I had to do lots of entertaining and I became a rounded business person. (Alison Carnwath, Chairman, Land Securities Group)

This additional visibility, however, also brings its own pressures. One of the interviewees talked about how one of her senior roles with an operational remit felt like being in a 'goldfish bowl', and how she became very visible during a restructure of her organization.

SUPPORT

One of the most important types of support a manager can give a woman is to take a risk and give her the opportunity to try her hand at an operational role. Mentors and sponsors have a role to play in highlighting the importance of operational roles to a woman early in her career. Where a woman has children and is in a general management role with significant travel requirements and emergency meetings, the 'village of support' that Ezzedeen and Ritchy talked about in Chapter 2 becomes important and has to be on stand-by to take care of children when the woman has urgent and unplanned work commitments to attend to.

TIMING

Operational experience, together with international experience, seems to be a critical job assignment that is best tackled early in a woman's career as it is easier to do this while there are no children, and because it also provides a woman with a great foundation for a later move to senior management:

> Operations experience is good to get early on as you will not be considered for the top job without it. The higher you are in a staff role the more difficult it is to get operations experience at the same level, as people are less willing to take a risk. This is advice I got from my former boss. (Hana Rolles, Head of Online Marketing and Sales, Vodafone Group)

The following comment provides a revealing insight into the challenges that women face when they are trying to gain operational experience:

> I was at a critical transition point. From a high-flying internal consulting role and change management role to an operations role which was important for my future career development but which was also fraught with potential pitfalls. I moved to another role and joined the development program to become a senior manager after

91

I returned from maternity leave. A senior manager had sponsored me to join the program, which was by invitation only. There were different views on what my next role should be. One of my senior managers felt that I should make a lateral move to a role where I could learn but also add value. On the other side, another senior director felt that I should take a role that was one level lower to further develop my knowledge of the market. He thought it would be too risky for the company if I made a lateral move as it would be a new way of working for me. It wasn't strategic and planning but day-to-day operations and delivery, with increased people management responsibilities. Coming back from maternity leave brought additional complexity to my move. One of my senior managers worried that I might be taking on too much – mother to a young child, the senior management development program and moving to operations. (Senior manager, FTSE 100 company)

A senior manager with a strong general management background made the following points about moving from a functional to an operational role:

How do you move from HR and marketing to running a P&L? Those who make the transition have to be very bright and have broader capabilities so that the organization is prepared to give them a chance. You need to be able to talk more broadly to the chief executive about the organisation and not just about your area. Nowadays there is the advantage of being able to declare that you want to go into broader roles during performance appraisal reviews. That was not the case years ago. (Senior manager, FTSE 100 company)

Before making a move to an operational role, it is helpful to be able to demonstrate broader commercial understanding. Functional expertise will not be enough to convince senior managers to give a woman a chance. Ways of broadening one's understanding of a business are sabbaticals, being a member of a cross-functional task force, or even extracurricular activities – for example, with a charity. Another senior manager shared her observations about the importance of project management experience, which can provide a good foundation for moving to operational roles and running parts of a business:

Running a business is very important in order to get a more senior role, but a good proxy for it is to run a large team or a complex project or program. They also deliver to the bottom line and they all provide you with a focus on results, commercial acumen, customer service, cost control, analytical thinking, intellectual challenge and the ability to influence others at a senior level. (Senior manager, FTSE 100 organization)

SUMMARY

Operational experience is key to progressing to the most senior roles in an organization. It is a great credibility builder and allows a woman to become visible in an organization through the very visible nature of the results she is delivering. However, operational roles come with many challenges, and some of these challenges are particularly women-specific, such as combining an often unplannable role with childcare responsibilities. There are also other challenges, such as having the nerve to ride out times of non-delivery and having to be comfortable with taking important decisions oneself. As women progress in an operational area, they will gain increasing responsibility for parts of a business, which brings with it the added complexity of looking after more than one functional area. Once this transition had been mastered, interviewees talked about the excitement and freedom of being able to 'run the show'. The In Focus section explored the challenges that women face when they are trying to combine an executive career with childcare responsibilities. Continuing at a 100 percent commitment level after having children comes at a great opportunity cost to one's family and requires a strong and extended support network. Juggling, and supportive husbands, are key to making it work. Senior management roles seem to provide some opportunity for flexibility, and the interviewees talked about their own strategies for making it all work. Extensive business travel, however, seems to be particularly difficult to accommodate in these finely-tuned schedules. As with the early stretch assignment and the international posting, operational experience is an experience to undertake early in a woman's career.

TAKING ACTION

- **Finding the right area.** Establish which parts of your organization's day-to-day operations appeal to you – sales, supply chain, production? If you are currently in a functional role, evaluate the operational area to which you could add most value in order to gain a level transfer or even a promotion.
- **Drawing on your existing experience.** What experience do you already have that will strengthen your case for a transfer to an operational role? Larger-scale people-management experience, significant project management experience or experience of integrating across different areas are valued by those who run a company's operations, as are a demonstration of resilience and the ability to perform effectively on 'alien turf'.
- **Your manager's support and concerns.** Let your manager and sponsor(s) know of your wish to gain operational experience. Giving you the opportunity to try your hand at an operational role will pose a risk for your manager too. Listen to his or her concerns in order to understand what types of assurance he or she needs to feel comfortable enough to take the risk.
- **Do you have enough support?** Will you need an extended network of support to help you deal with unplanned travel and emergency meetings? Establish who can provide this assistance.

7

PEOPLE MANAGEMENT RESPONSIBILITY: BUILDING A HIGH-PERFORMANCE TEAM

To succeed you need to be able to deliver and to do that you need to build a great team.
(Cathryn Riley, UK Commercial Director, Aviva)

Start as you mean to go on. Be overly convincing. If you are leading the meeting, go into the meeting leading.
(Monique Dumas, Investor Relations and Corporate Communications Partner, Electra Partners)

Leading a small team is often the first step up the career ladder and for many women it represents a big step from being a sole contributor to delivering through others. With increasing levels of seniority, people management moves from managing people in relatively stable environments to managing them through particular challenges such as organizational change and crises. While acknowledged repeatedly by the interviewees as being core to their success, people management was only mentioned as a critical job assignment in two cases. In all other situations, it emerged as a secondary feature to other critical job assignments such as running a large manufacturing plant abroad, executing large-scale organizational change or turning round a failing operation. This is not surprising, as senior managers are expected to deliver results by harnessing the energies of the team they are leading. People management presents its own challenges, but once mastered, the team should act as a source of support rather than as the main challenge to be tackled. Since effective people management is so crucial to being able to deal with almost all of the other critical job assignments in this book, I have decided to devote a separate chapter to the topic even though it did not emerge as a stand-alone critical job assignment during the interviews.

Charan and colleagues highlight the transition from sole contributor to manager, and then again from manager to become the manager of managers, as being among the most critical transition points along a leader's path and one that often leads to problems if the transition is not made successfully.[1] The first transition, from sole contributor to team manager, is often not taken easily as new managers continue to do the work of their teams rather than focusing solely on managing the team; they have yet to learn to deliver through others. If they continue to do what they were good at as a sole contributor they will frustrate their team with their over-involvement and are unlikely to have enough time to focus on planning the team's work and on developing the team. Building a high-performance team is an important skill for any woman and will help her to master the various critical job assignments she will encounter as she progresses in her career.

With a manager's increasing seniority, the size of her team also tends to get bigger, and she will become a manager of managers, which adds further complexity to people management. What constitutes a large team depends on whether a woman is in a functional role, where a team of 100 is considered large, or in an operational role, where a team of 300–400 people or more is the norm. This is an important distinction, as managing large teams of hundreds, if not thousands, of people is often regarded as one of the credentials that allows a woman to demonstrate her leadership potential. Interestingly, though, a number of the interviewees, including those with a general management background, indicated that large-scale people management may not be as vital as is sometimes stated provided other types of challenges, such as dealing with crises or other forms of complexity, have been mastered: 'If you have credibility then you can skip a few steps – large-scale people management is one of them' (Senior manager, FTSE 100 company).

Nevertheless, large-scale people management experience is clearly a formative experience and brings its own challenges. When a manager is responsible for a large number of people, she is often in charge of delivering the products and services of an organization directly, hence the success of her management skills will have a direct impact on the organization's success. The change from a team leader to a manager of managers completes the transition from technical expertise to management; while team managers assess their team with regard to technical knowledge and technical delivery, managers of managers assess their direct team with regard to how they manage their people.

JOB-SPECIFIC CHALLENGES

All the job-specific challenges of people management center on building a high-performance team which allows a woman to deliver outstanding results for the organization.

Building a strong and direct team

A strong, direct, team is the backbone to every woman's career success. Only if the entire team is 'singing from the same hymn sheet' can outstanding results be achieved. Building a strong, direct team involves a number of different elements, such as understanding individuals' strengths and weaknesses, making changes to the team to get the best out of people, creating a team environment where everyone works together, being clear about what is expected, and supporting the team through coaching and development initiatives. The following comments illustrate the importance of this multifaceted approach to building a strong team:

> Be clear about success. Support, coach, motivate and set high standards. I only ask others to do things that I would do myself. If the team succeeds, then everyone in it succeeds. I put a lot of effort into developing my team. (Cathryn Riley, UK Commercial Director, Aviva)

> I had to create an environment where everyone got on in the team and where the team pulled together. There could be no more back-biting. I had to line people up behind my new strategy. (Senior manager, FTSE 100 company)

> I have always had a good team. I have always worked out quickly what people's strengths are and I have always made changes along the way. I have no qualms about restructuring. I couldn't have done it alone. (Senior manager, FTSE 100 company)

Sorting out people problems

Sorting out existing people problems is an integral part of building a high-performing team. Leaving such problems unaddressed means that a manager cannot rely on the team to complete important day-to-day tasks in an effective and high-quality manner. As a result, constant problem-fixing distracts the manager from the strategic, forward-looking activities in which she should be engaging. A number of the senior interviewees recognized the importance of addressing people problems swiftly:

> Sorting out people issues is essential for a leader – all CEOs I have worked with have regretted not sorting out people issues earlier as it damages businesses. (HR director, FTSE 100 company)

> Sorting out people problems is critical. A leader is supposed to lead people forward. Not all good managers are good leaders, but all good leaders are good managers. You need to sort out underperformance. (Claire Jenkins, Group Director, Corporate Affairs, Rexam)

One senior manager pointed to the added complexities often encountered in modern workplaces which makes it all the more important to address people issues:

> Sorting out people problems has become more important because of different generations working together and the increase in matrix structures in organizations. In this context you need agile working patterns and be able to use different leadership styles. (Senior manager, FTSE 100 company)

Managers who take on a new area or a new team may be tempted to delay sorting out issues in their teams because of a desire to give the existing team the benefit of the doubt, as well as the managers' reliance on their inherited team to gain vital knowledge about their new area.[2] As this section showed, however, such delays can reduce the manager's ability to deliver much-needed results.

Engaging people

Once people problems are addressed and a strong team is built, the next task of a people manager is to ensure that the team is fully engaged and in support of the manager's strategy. Creating engagement for large teams can be a particularly difficult challenge. Dictating action to others rarely achieves the desired outcomes; in the best case it will lead to coercion, and in the worst case to resistance. A McKinsey survey showed that non-financial sources of motivation such as praise from one's managers, opportunities to have one-to-one conversations with leaders, or the opportunity to take on a significant project can significantly increase an employee's motivation levels.[3] McMahon goes even further and points to the importance of building a dialogue and of creating a bedrock of shared meaning underpinning the team as they face various challenges together:[4]

> There had been 100 people in the team; 60 had been made redundant and 40 demoralized people were left. I had to do something with them ... I had managed up to 200 people before, which is a real strength for me. With this team I had to look to the future, develop a new strategy and get the team involved in this process. We had a launch event and I ensured that all the issues were aired and addressed. I gained the team's trust. (Senior manager, FTSE 100 company)

> In this role I managed 500 people. I had to engage them around the challenges and give them a part in the solution. I am an honest and upfront leader, and people trust me. I gave others the confidence to develop more than just a pedestrian function and I showed them how to be seen as a true business partner. To achieve this I set the team's KPIs [key performance indicators], I trained and developed them and provided support. (HR director, FTSE 100 organization)

One challenge that emerged specifically with regard to managing a large team was how to reach not only one's immediate management team but also how to find ways to engage hundreds or even thousands of people in both a time-effective way and without alienating the middle managers. A number of interviewees from a general management background talked in more detail about this challenge, for example:

> How do you manage a large number of people? You need to think about your communication. How can you reach a large number of people directly and not always via your direct reports? I get around the business to meet people and I see groups of people and managers, but I make sure my direct reports don't feel compromised. (Jessica Burley, CEO, MCHI)

Delegating to gain headroom

Learning to trust others and letting them deliver something that you are ultimately held responsible for means relinquishing control and learning to be a key player without doing everything yourself. It is an important challenge to come to terms with, and a number of the interviewees described how they had to learn to deal with this challenge by clearly defining their own role within the team.

> It was difficult to let go after I had stepped into the delegation role. I needed to get the trust to let them do it and had to make myself allow them to make mistakes. I had to allow them to be successful in their own right. What helped me was to take on other things that complement my role. I have given myself the role of the political one who does the lobbying. That is helpful to the strategy that the team and I were pursuing. (Senior manager, property industry)

Don't be afraid to assume authority

Authority is an important part of establishing oneself as a leader. It has to be won by building trust with a new team; there is also a strong element of self-confidence involved.[5] Ruderman and Ohlott followed high-achieving career women at different stages of their careers for one year, and one of the challenges they talk about is women's hesitation to assume authority as part of a managerial career.[6] For women in particular, holding a position of authority may be more difficult initially as women are still taught to get on with others and to be supportive. Evans highlights that women often accept additional responsibilities but are less ready to accept additional authority. But as women move up in organizations they need authority to be able to deal with increasingly challenging problems:[7]

> My team are all older than me. Other people are often surprised. Some are older by ten years. I was initially more conscious of it than they were. For most it's not an issue, but for one team member it *is* an issue. It is not explicit, but this person thinks I lack knowledge due to the age difference. I had to push back and deal with it head on and learn to get the best out of this person. I have been role playing with my coach to help me deal with the situation. (Senior manager, FTSE 100 company)

100

Trust your instincts when you are making decisions and position yourself at the beginning as you would like to carry on. Don't be too understated early on. (Anna Capitanio, Vice-President, Organizational Effectiveness and M&A HR, BT Global Services)

Learning to deal with these challenges is important for women. It has been shown that not being able to delegate, build a team or empower others can make the transition to more senior roles difficult, and increasingly act as a derailer for leaders.[8]

There are three additional people management challenges that emerged during the interviews. I have, however, decided to deal with these in different chapters. These are: managing geographically dispersed teams, which is explored in Chapter 5; leading people through change which is examined in Chapter 10; and leading people in times of crises which is discussed in Chapter 11.

WOMEN-SPECIFIC CHALLENGES

Women as managers

Studies that involve managers in real work settings rather than non-work simulation experiments find less pronounced differences between the genders than are often reported.[9] Nevertheless, there are important, if subtle, differences between the ways that men and women manage and lead people. Women tend to display a more democratic leadership style, whereas men use a more autocratic style. A McKinsey study found that women engaged in more people development activities, role modelled more frequently and used expectations and rewards more often than did their male counterparts.[10] They also demonstrated inspirational behaviour and participative decision-making somewhat more than male managers. Men, on the other hand, used more control and corrective action along with individualistic decision-making. While women's leadership style is increasingly being praised as being more effective, Carli and Eagly report that successful women merge female traits of warmth with male traits of taking action in order to be effective and not to create friction and alienation with their male counterparts.[11] However, in very male-dominated environments this blending approach does not seem to work. In this case the only way to succeed is for the woman to become 'one of the boys' and to adopt a male leadership style. The Institute of Leadership and Management

(ILM) found that employees report slightly more trust in people who have a similar background to them. Women use their competence and provide support when they manage men in order to address this slight disadvantage in perceived trust:[12]

LESSONS LEARNED

Making diversity work

Everyone in a team has to feel valued as an individual to be fully committed to the team's goals and genuinely engaged. In addition to creating a shared vision and building joint meaning, managers need to demonstrate a clear understanding of every person as an individual, together with their strengths and desires. A good manager is flexible in her leadership style and recognizes that her team's working styles and approaches may be different than her own. Managing diverse teams can come at a price, as one senior manager in the financial industry pointed out:

'[Organizations] want diversity but it makes it more difficult if people have different backgrounds and different working styles, as everyone approaches things differently. There is an implementation cost to putting in place diverse teams' (Senior manager, finance industry).

A number of the interviewees talked about how they had learned to appreciate differences; taking time to listen to others is an integral part of this process, as the following comments show:

This role taught me to be empathetic and see issues from others' points of view. I learned to spend time with others to learn about their issues. (Senior manager, FTSE 100 company)

[In this role] I learned about people management. It taught me to work with a diverse group of people, from the ambitious graduate to contractors. I learned about different styles. (Jo Pisani, Partner, PricewaterhouseCoopers)

Creating genuine engagement

The interviewees learned about effective ways of creating engagement through their personal experience of feeling engaged or disengaged.

They also talked about adopting a 'winning hearts and minds' approach:

> I changed from being an intellectual, financial person into a practical, hearts-and-minds person. I used my financial experience to prioritize. I can now act like an extrovert; I have learned to talk to people at all levels, winning hearts and minds. I have also learned to chit-chat and appreciate that everybody is different. I am listening; telling people off doesn't work. I have learned how you get people to believe in you and how to find people's strengths so you can help them to excel. I now continually stress the importance of strengths. If you have self-belief you can turn things around. (Senior manager, FTSE 100 company)

> I managed a team of 60 direct and 60 indirect reports based around the world. I managed to get it to the point where people who didn't work for me directly volunteered to chair some of my team meetings. Learning to harness the energy of people who didn't work for me helped me develop leadership through influence rather than purely through my position. (Karen Oddey, CEO of an equity funded specialist electronics company)

> I have learned my leadership skills from my managers. I learned from great leaders who demonstrated how powerful it was to feel like being part of a hand-picked team. That was a great contrast to before, where I had witnessed bad leadership … which has made me think about the impact of bad leadership. (Senior manager, finance industry)

IN FOCUS: ROLE MODELS

In addition to supportive partners, supportive managers and sponsors, role models are the fourth category of significant others that play an important part in a woman's career. Role models are usually more senior people in a similar organizational setting to our own, from whom we learn by observing and modelling their values, behaviors and actions. Female role models can show more junior women how to have successful corporate careers. They are however rare, which is a problem that has a significant impact on

---

women's career progression. The lack of female role models means that women often find it more difficult to work out how to behave in an organization, especially in a male-dominated one. It may also make it harder for women to see what routes to the top may work for them, particularly when they have to balance work and family commitments. As a result, women may be less sure of whether the route to the top is feasible at all. The following comments show what impact a lack of female role models can have:

> Only 10 percent of the consultants were women, so there were no role models as to how to behave. (Hana Rolles, Head of Online Marketing and Sales, Vodafone Group)

> We don't have many female role models so you need to find your own path. Maybe that is why it takes longer for women to get there. (Karen Dolenec, Financial Managing Director, Terra Firma Capital Partners)

> I am not a role model as I didn't have children and was 110 percent committed and travelled like crazy. It is very difficult for women with children. They don't want an easy ride but if they look up and cannot see anyone at the top that is hard. (Senior manager, finance industry)

In contrast, in situations where women do have female role models, the benefits they gain are significant. One interviewee even pointed out that she chose one particular project assignment over another as she felt that the female case leader was a great role model. The benefits of role models range from learning about effective strategies and dealing with difficult situations to opening a woman's eyes to alternative ways of being successful while maintaining her authenticity. The following comment from a senior executive in a FTSE 100 company illustrates this last point very well:

> My boss was a woman and she did the role differently from all other men in that role before. I thought 'If she can do it, why not me? I can do this role differently, too.' It clarified the path to the top for me. I could relate to my boss as she is a woman and it helped me to come to terms with my ambition. (Anna Capitanio, Vice-President, Organizational Effectiveness and M&A HR, BT Global Services)

Role models make a lot of difference. Women meet other women and learn that you don't have to lose your identity to be successful. You can be authentic but you may need to work in a slightly different manner. (Senior manager, FTSE 100 company)

A number of the interviewees talked about how they valued male role models, as they helped them to broaden their own leadership style:

Role models have made a huge difference to me. I have had two female role models and all the others have been male. I learned from one male role model about being very clear and decisive. He could be directive but he was also able to change himself and his opinions. He grew to understand the importance of people investment and invested in his own team. (Senior manager, finance industry)

A number of the interviewees also talked about becoming role models themselves and being an inspiration to other women. The following comment is a great illustration of this:

When I worked in manufacturing we had to wear a cap when we were going on the shop floor. They had different coloured bands to denote seniority. There were only about ten senior women in a staff of 1,500. I was the most senior. I would often forget to take my cap and just take a fresh plain white cap out of the basket on the shop floor. The women on the shop floor approached me and asked me to wear my coloured cap. They were very supportive of me. (Senior manager, FTSE 100 company).

Two interviewees in particular stood out as role models. They clearly demonstrated that organizational approaches can be adapted effectively to ensure outstanding organizational performance as well as levelling the playing field for the women in their teams. These women acted not only as role models but also as creative and innovative champions of women. One senior interviewee, a member of her organization's executive committee, talked about how she had provided round-the-clock cover for her various clients across the world while at the same time creating a truly flexible work structure. One woman, for example, comes in later by one or two hours every morning, which allows her to drop her children off at school. In exchange, she comes in on Saturday mornings, when her husband is at home, to provide some of the department's weekend cover. Another woman works a number of additional hours every day to cover the early morning shift and in exchange takes one afternoon a week off to allow her to accommodate some of her commitments outside of work. Another interviewee, Helen Mahy, Company Secretary & General Counsel at National Grid, talked about how flexible recruitment solutions in her organization have helped women get roles as the best candidate:

> We interviewed for a senior job in a technical area. A woman candidate was the best but she lacked technical experience. So we restructured the job, took out the technical elements and gave her the management responsibility. Another woman works three days a week and we gave her a great assistant so that we have cover five days per week. And it was a step up for him too. With women you have to be more imaginative.

Taking action sooner

As we saw earlier in this chapter, women's leadership style is often characterized by listening, cooperation and consultation. However, as women become more senior they increasingly face critical job assignments that require immediate action, fast decisions and clear direction. The following comments the interviewees made about taking action to give their teams certainty and direction are probably also a reflection of women learning the value of a more directive leadership style in certain situations as they take on more senior roles:

> I would have made some decisions earlier on as some people need direction and not too much consultation. (HR director, FTSE 100 company)

> The people [management] piece is important. I am down-to-earth, I know the difference between right and wrong and I am not scared to speak out. If things don't work out, I don't hang around – I change things. I don't dwell on it and just sort it out. I bring focus and pace [to the team]. (Senior manager, finance industry)

My natural style of leadership is highly participative. However, I found that as the scale of my role increased, or when the team didn't have the same level of ability or experience, I had to develop a more directive approach. One colleague explained it as having to 'grab the bull by the horns'. This experience certainly helped me to develop a wider set of leadership styles to use. (CEO, UK company)

This lesson allows women to balance their participative leadership style with more directive elements of leadership, and this helps them to become a more credible contender for senior roles. There will be more about taking action in Chapter 11, when the challenges of dealing with problems and crises are explored.

CAREER BENEFITS

Creating a high-performance work environment

As mentioned earlier, the interviewees talked about people management as a secondary challenge in connection with other critical job assignments such as projects involving turnaround or organizational change. Nevertheless, there seems to be one important career-enhancing benefit from managing people effectively that is widely acknowledged: building a high-performance environment. It is about demonstrating to others that, as a leader, a woman can build an environment that allows people to work to their full potential:

I motivated the team and made sure that everybody believed in the vision. I demonstrated passion about the project. I improved internal communications and reached out to other departments by setting up regular meetings and therefore moved people from escalation mode to communication mode. (Paola Cuneo, General Manager, BT)

I managed to drive consistent growth and to create a good working environment where people want to work. My group is seen as smart, proactive and strategic. It is also flexible and can tackle many different problems, and we have built good client relationships. (Senior manager, FTSE 100 company)

The company runs staff feedback surveys. My function's scores were 30 percent higher than other functions. I had lots of heads of function talk to me about how I had achieved this. My function was the only function that was consistently green across all areas. (Senior manager, FTSE 100 company)

Delivering results time and again

Very closely linked to setting up a high-performance work environment is the actual delivery of results, which is highly valued by organizations. One senior manager mentioned that, in today's business environment, people are forgiven almost anything but not non-delivery. Delivering results is one of the topics mentioned by almost every interviewee. How did you get ahead? What is the secret to your success? What is the one piece of advice you would pass on to other women? The answer to all these questions was frequently 'deliver':

Deliver results as they get you noticed. (HR director, FTSE 100 company)

Produce results and don't let anything get between you and the sales, but don't trample over people in the process. (CEO, UK company)

Always deliver. People will see through you eventually if you don't. (Senior manager, FTSE 100 company)

And this is very much what good people management will allow a woman leader to do time and again: deliver results. Many of the interviewees stated clearly that without their teams they would not have been able to deliver.

SUPPORT

A manager can support a new team leader or a new manager of managers by being a good role model and by recognizing the challenges that new people managers face. When it comes to developing people management skills, learning from others is very powerful and the most common form of learning described by the interviewees. We learn from both good and less good bosses. Experiencing what bad people management feels like is how some of the interviewees learned what not to do. Hill points to the importance of bosses recognizing that a new manager or a new manager of managers will initially struggle with the transition.[13] Recognizing this and making clear to the new manager that it is acceptable to seek support can help to alleviate the isolation that new managers may feel, and will reduce their reluctance to seek help for fear of appearing insecure or inexperienced.

TIMING

While being a team manager is a challenge that is useful to try to tackle early in one's career, managing large numbers of people may require more maturity and may best be left to a later stage, as the following two comments show.

> I was responsible for a lot of people who were older than me early on in my career. But I am not afraid to be heard and I am a sociable person. I have also been given a lot of challenging jobs early on, such as having to make a lot of people redundant. Now I am not fazed by very much due to this early exposure. It has equipped me to deal with most things and I now have good knowledge of all the issues as I started dealing with them early on. (Senior manager, FTSE 100 company)

> Don't do large-scale people management too early. You need experience and maturity. Your decision-making needs to be matured in order to deal with the complexity of a large team. (Anna Capitanio, Vice-President, Organizational Effectiveness and M&A HR, BT Global Services)

SUMMARY

People management is key to a woman's success. The more senior a woman becomes and the grittier the roles she has to master, the more important her team becomes. Realizing that you cannot do it yourself is an important insight. While large-scale people management may not be critical for every woman, particularly those who progress in functional roles, demonstrating that you can manage hundreds if not thousands of people effectively is a great confirmation that a manager can deal with scope and complexity. Building a strong, immediate team, sorting out people problems and learning to feel comfortable with authority provide a woman with headroom. It allows her to employ her team to deal with day-to-day problems so she can focus on bigger-picture problems, senior-level lobbying and forward planning. As one senior manager put it earlier, only if everyone is singing from the same hymn sheet can true results be achieved, and it is these results that organizations and senior managers value. People management is a good experience to have early in one's career, but only on a smaller scale. Large-scale people management is complex and requires a certain level of maturity to be able to deal with it effectively.

TAKING ACTION

- **Get support.** If you are in the process of making the transition from being a sole contributor to a team manager, or from there to becoming a manager of managers, recognize the significance of this transition. It is often underplayed and new managers are left with too little support. Effective people management skills are the key to senior people's success. Discuss any of your challenges with your own manager to help you become an effective people manager as soon as possible.
- **Learn from others**. If you are already established in a people management role, evaluate your effectiveness by considering how strongly engaged your team is, and how conducive the work environment you have created is to delivering outstanding results. Take a closer look at senior managers around you who are examples of good and less good leadership. How do you compare, and how can you further improve?
- **Be confident.** Effective people management not only requires a good grasp of people's strengths and the ability to run effective performance reviews with your team, it also requires the confidence to take action, give direction and assume authority. Giving direction should not be confused with being dictatorial. Authority cannot be demanded but has to be earned; nevertheless, personal confidence will allow you to lead your team effectively should times become more turbulent and uncertain.

8

WORKING IN A DIFFERENT ENVIRONMENT: NEW ROLES, NEW FUNCTIONS AND NEW INDUSTRIES

If you have only one channel to market then your opportunities and approaches are limited. Moving to different environments is challenging but also hugely rewarding.

(Jessica Burley, CEO, MCHI)

If you are open to new experiences and curious then things will come to you. You have to deliver, take responsibility and do additional things such as secondments and committee work. Give people the confidence that you can do things and that you are an all-rounder.

(Margaret Johnson, Group CEO, Leagas Delaney)

It is tempting to stay in a familiar environment. The area where we 'grew up' and learned our trade is well-known to us. We understand its culture and know how to get things done. While change is disruptive, it seems to be the price we have to be willing to pay for true learning. Only if we move outside our comfort zone is our thinking challenged and we are forced to learn new ways of doing things. If a woman wants to progress in her career she needs to understand how the different parts of the organization link together. She also has to understand the organization's competing needs and be able to see an issue from different perspectives in order to make the best decision overall, rather than just for one particular function:

The same set of experiences time and time again is not useful, you need to completely change the context and get out of your comfort zone. It is not so much an issue of whether you are in line or functional roles, it is more about how often you are in a new context

111

and a new sector and new roles. It is the *change* in job roles that is important. For example, it is important to be part of an acquisition, both while acquiring and while being acquired, and it is important to be in a situation where money has been lost and to have worked in a low-margin environment. (HR director, FTSE 100 company)

All interviewees recognized the importance of having a broad base to their careers. A number of them talked about how they took conscious steps to broaden their experience base, as the following comments show:

I took the conscious decision to broaden out. I joined a management consultancy where I could work in different sectors. It was a pivotal change for me. I started and then specialized in financial services, which was new to me. I had exposure to broader projects, such as cost reduction projects and change projects. They were multidisciplinary; for example, treasury and IT. I was sent on long overseas assignments to Eastern Europe and Saudi Arabia. This time allowed me to broaden my international experience. (Cathryn Riley, UK Commercial Director, Aviva)

[After eight years in retail] I went to McKinsey as an experienced industry hire and helped to set up their retail practice. I decided to take the role as it is a big brand and it would help me to fill in my analytical skills. It would give me CFO exposure. I felt like a fish out of water as McKinsey is quite formal, analytical and has a long-hours culture. But I made some of my best friends there. It gave me the ability to never be frightened about anything. It taught me how to disaggregate problems. It was a lovely culture where people helped each other. (Helen Buck, Convenience Director, Sainsbury)

This chapter will explore three broad types of changes to one's established work environment. First, the interviewees talked about the challenges (and associated learning) of moving to a significantly different role but staying in the same function, the same organization and the same industry. Moving to a different role in this case does not mean a promotion from, say, an account executive post to that of account manager; it involves a real step change. One interviewee, for example, talked about moving from a research role to a commercial role.

Second, the interviewees talked about staying in the same role but moving to a different organization, and often also to a different industry sector. A woman may stay in her role as a senior operations manager, for example, but move from one organization to another. A number of the interviewees also talked about moving to a more senior role in their area of expertise in a new company and a new industry. These moves were often experienced as a big step up. The role itself was significantly more senior, which was further exacerbated by a move to an unfamiliar organization and an unfamiliar industry. Charan and colleagues point out that the step from being a manager of managers to becoming a functional manager, for example, is a big one. While the function remains the same, the woman is suddenly responsible for the entire range of units that fall under the function's umbrella. An IT department, for example, tends to include areas of expertise as diverse as telephony, networks and servers, user support, disaster recovery and business continuity. These moves require a manager to consider multiple perspectives and to make decisions for the greater good of the function rather than for just one specific area. This requires thinking like a business person rather than merely a functionary.[1] The interviewees described these times as tough and talked about working incredibly long hours to become familiar with the new environment. They also talked about spending every waking hour on building new relationships and learning about the new business model.

The final type of work environment change this chapter explores is arguably the most difficult; it is the move from one functional area to another. A woman may move from an operational role at a manufacturing plant to a center of expertise role at head office, or vice versa – she may move from an internal consulting or strategy role to an operational role. A precursor to working in a different department may be to join an inter-departmental working group as a way of getting a flavour of what concerns other departments have and to make contacts. Many moves to a different function may mean a lateral rather than an upward move. Ideally, a move will allow the woman to bring valued skills from her current function to the new function and apply it there to a new customer base, new markets and generally new processes. McCall and colleagues talk about their interviewees being 'on alien turf' when they had switched from operational to functional roles.[2] Moving from operational to functional roles or vice versa normally also includes a physical relocation: from an operational site to head office or the reverse. These cross-functional moves, particularly from a functional to an operational role, become increasingly difficult as a person becomes more senior, as we saw in the previous chapter.

Across these three situations, women have to get to grips with new types of customers, markets, stakeholders, business models and much more. These experiences can make a woman feel 'like a fish out of water'. All require some significant adaptation of personal working styles and learning to operate in a new environment with different rules of engagement.

The interviewees considered that moving to a new role, function or industry was the most frequently encountered critical job assignment. Interestingly, though, it is an area we don't read so much about. Changing to a new work environment is seen as something people just do. Nevertheless, there are a number of challenges associated with it.

JOB-SPECIFIC CHALLENGES

A steep learning curve

Learning about a new function or industry covers many different elements, such as learning about products that are different and possibly complex, decoding different terminology and jargon, and generally getting to terms with being a novice again and learning the ropes. Many of the interviewees talked about the need to learn fast and to make an impact quickly in order to establish credibility. Often, no training and little support were provided in the new role. Many interviewees talked about how they toured the business to learn more, how they talked to different people across the organization to increase their understanding, and how they spent many hours familiarizing themselves with new information. A small number of the women mentioned how reporting back to their bosses about their meetings and tours of the business was a good way also for their boss to stay in touch with different parts of the business. Finally, a number of the interviewees mentioned the importance of being seen to be helpful while they were establishing themselves in the new function or industry; they went beyond the remit of their roles in order to add value where they could.

> I didn't know anything about marketing and after a few weeks my manager was fired and I replaced him. I was 23 years old and hadn't received any training or support so I had to learn on the job. I had to decide what to do and then get on with it … I needed the confidence to stick my neck out. (Mary Lawrance, Owner of Cariance Executive Search)

I moved to a director role in my mid-thirties. In this role I had the responsibility of getting new work. You always have to build new skills sets. It was a big step up from the previous role, where I did not have to bring in new work. The organization had lots of existing clients but losing clients was also career limiting. I had to find new clients. It was very daunting and competitive. Until then I had been working on the analysis side and it was a real step change in role. However, I find it easy to get in the door and to talk to people. I had to present ideas persuasively and had to go out and be an order-maker and not wait and be an order-taker. (Alison Carnwath, Chairman, Land Securities Group)

As we saw in Chapter 4, Dotlich and colleagues point out that realizing that you don't know what you need to know is one of the most painful discoveries during a stretch assignment. They highlight the danger of reacting to these situations with a lack of flexibility, and by relying on one's existing problem-solving repertoire. Instead, listening and asking questions increases the capacity to adapt and allows people to find new ways to be effective in new situations.[3] To overcome a lack of knowledge, the interviewees often talked about working long hours to get to grips with their new environment and its challenges.

I was allowed to take on a new challenge. It opened my mind to change and I learned new things. I had to get on with it. It was a very stressful time and I had to rise to the pressure and stay level-headed. The challenge was dealing with the workload. Everything was new and I was working until 3am to get the work done. My initial achievements were recognized, which built my confidence: 'I can do this'. I was given a promotion after nine months. (Senior manager, FTSE 100 company)

A new culture and different expectations

Most often, the move to a new organization brings with it a new culture that has to be decoded. The interviewees talked about having to work out, for example, how much stakeholder management was expected, or what senior management's general expectations were. Here is what one senior manager said after she had moved to a global company in a different industry: 'I flew to the US to a conference, not knowing what to expect. There were 25,000 people in a football stadium and

I had to speak for the UK' (Kate Bostock, Executive Director, General Merchandise, Marks & Spencer).

McCall and colleagues, who interviewed mainly operational managers, reported that one of the main frustrations of their interviewees' moves to functional roles was the sudden lack of being able to demonstrate their impact on the bottom line, and being rewarded for their input rather than their output. It took them some time to get used to this new way of measuring performance. Not being able to show sales or production numbers made these managers feel as though they were not doing a real job. The women I interviewed who had made a similar move also talked about the need to readjust. They learned about the importance of persuasion and presenting information in the absence of concrete numbers:

> I moved from an operational into a conceptual role. It took me longer than usual to settle into the role. There were different ways of measuring success – from an output-focused success model in my operational roles to now being rewarded for my inputs and thinking. I felt that the role was not right for me but my boss convinced me to give it another go. I stuck it out and did the job for a few more years. Once I had overcome the initial problems with the new way of working the role turned out to be pivotal for me. It gave me confidence that I can deliver just as successfully as a conceptual thinker as an operational deliverer. The experience from this role formed one of the pillars for a move to a senior role later on, where I took a company through a time of real adversity. (HR director, FTSE 100 company)

Establishing credibility

The interviewees who had moved from functional to operational roles often talked about establishing credibility as being their biggest challenge and about how they encountered technical experts, often older and more senior men, who were dismissive of what they might be able to contribute. Moving to a new function, a completely new role or a different industry is often accompanied by the cynicism of established local experts:

> Credibility initially was a problem and it was only through developing a relationship with the senior director that I got an honest

answer and good insights. Often senior managers don't give honest answers, and only say 'OK' because they don't want to take the time to explain how things really work as they think that you will not add value and will not stick around for too long. They started to look at me with more respect when I demonstrated that I wanted to learn, that I was hard working, persistent and honest, and that I was able to apply what I had learned from them both in terms of vision and factual knowledge. I became an ambassador for their ideas across the organization. (Middle manager, FTSE 100 company)

I held executive responsibility for the first time [in this role]. I looked after the branch network which were operations units with P&L. I had to gain the team's and colleagues' credibility. I had an unusual background – human resources – rather than the usual progression in the branch all the way to branch manger. Some branch managers threatened to leave but the board supported me. I was relatively young, female and had not done my time in the branch network. There were credibility issues but I learned how to gain credibility and manage a geographically-dispersed team of 2,000 people in diverse functions. I demonstrated broader leadership skills. (Cathryn Riley, UK Commercial Director, Aviva)

A lack of credibility makes the delivery of results very difficult, if not impossible. A number of the interviewees also talked about the added challenge of not only being new to the area themselves but also the role they were taking on being new to the organization or function. This creates similar challenges to those explored in Chapter 9. These challenges are mainly about devising a strategy for the new role or function, convincing others of that strategy, finding allies and implementing the strategy effectively for quick returns:

I went into a new area. It was all very new for me and also a new role for the organization. I had to persuade others to buy into my plans for the role and I had to convince them to do something new that they would see as administration. I had to develop an understanding for what they were after and build relationships. I had to understand the business and their issues so I could deliver solutions. (Senior manager, FTSE 100 company)

Building new relationships

A new role with a completely different focus brings with it new stakeholders and so does a move to a different function or a different industry. Relationships have to be built in order to get work done. The interviewees talked in particular about the importance of building relationships with senior managers in the organization:

> I had a blank piece of paper as to what to achieve in the new function. Shortly afterwards I was also asked to pick two other areas which were new for me. This was also the first time I reported to an operations director. I had always reported to finance before ... He was different from the finance directors I had reported to before. He was more competitive and was not office based. I learned to feed into his competitive style. (Senior manager, FTSE 100 company)

As McCall and colleagues highlight, moving to head office often exposes women to some of the most senior managers in the organization. Equally, moving from functional roles to operational roles often means moving away from frequent access to senior management, as the following comment shows:

'Staff roles often have access to the CEO. In P&L roles, on the other hand, you are out with the troops and often have limited access to senior people' (Mary Lawrance, Founder of Cariance Executive Search).

The different working environments are likely to influence the working style of the new stakeholders with whom a woman has to build relationships. The global, strategic outlook of head office may feel very different than the day-to-day focus of a local operational unit.

Before moving on to exploring some of the women-specific challenges that the interviewees talked about, I would like to share one more comment which illustrates how the different challenges women encounter when they move to a new environment require resilience and tenacity:

> You need resilience and confidence. I am currently feeling like I am walking through mud. You need to keep on fighting. On the outside I am showing energy and on the inside it's tough. I have learned about the power of having the right people support me. I have learned how to make things happen and how to get a whole organization moving. (Middle manager, FTSE 100 organization)

WOMEN-SPECIFIC CHALLENGES

A journey of self-discovery

Women's additional challenges do not always result from the outside world, though many do, as we have already seen, and as we shall see more of in subsequent chapters. Some of the challenges women face are linked to the journeys of self-discovery they have to complete in order to become well-rounded leaders. Let us take a look at what a number of the interviewees had to say. This first comment is a great illustration of how a senior leader found her unique leadership style:

> I had to acquire gravitas. I spent time to figure out what stature meant for me. I had to work out how to take my conclusions and deliver them with more calmness, assertiveness and presence ... to demonstrate that I know what I am talking about. I had to work out how to be taken seriously as a leader. (Margaret Johnson, CEO, Leagas Delaney)

A middle manager talked about the challenges of being her own worst critic, and about learning to find the confidence to operate in large meetings:

> I am my own worst critic and I keep analysing what I am doing. Sometimes I am quiet in meetings and say nothing as I feel I have nothing worth adding. But then somebody else says the exact thing I had in mind and I regret not saying it. I also feel that in large groups it's harder for me to gauge reactions and to get feedback. I feel more comfortable when I get feedback in a one-to-one meeting. I am happy to share information and my opinions in large meetings if it is part of my remit. If it is not my area I feel that I have to add value such as sharing knowledge that others don't know about or input that will shape the conversation. (Middle manager, FTSE 100 company)

Another senior manager talked about her attempts to find a leadership style that worked both for herself and for the organization. She explained how she had received the feedback she needed to become more of a leader and take charge in large meetings, with mainly men attending. After using a more directive style, she then received feedback that she was perceived as unapproachable. She worked out that, while she needed to be more directive in meetings to demonstrate leadership qualities, her senior managers were expecting her to counterbalance this more directive approach with a softer and more personal approach before and after meetings.

IN FOCUS: INTEGRITY AND CULTURAL FIT

A concept that is often talked about in relation to women in business is integrity. Women value integrity and see it as one of their guiding principles, and it seems to become increasingly important as women get older.[4] This study was no different, and integrity – and loosely related to it, cultural fit – emerged as strong drivers for the interviewees. A small number of the interviewees recalled experiences where they walked away from significant job opportunities to maintain their integrity:

> This was the toughest time of my life. I had problems with the senior leadership and quit. I struggled with the lack of integrity. I was asked to stay and was offered any role that I might want. I felt that this could put me in a difficult position later on, as I could be asked for a favour [in return]. It was the most career-limiting move for me. I thought 'What have I done!' But looking back, it was the right thing to do. (Senior manager, FTSE 100 company)

When the senior managers were asked what they felt their bosses saw in them, one of the more frequently mentioned qualities was honesty and integrity.

As was seen in the In Focus section in Chapter 7, the overwhelming majority of interviewees, and particularly those with children, talked about the sacrifices and the opportunity cost of their careers to their lives. It is therefore perhaps not surprising to hear that women place much value on integrity. One senior manager said:

> I cannot work in an environment without integrity. Emotionally I just cannot do that. I know what I am prepared to accept, and what not. I have a little boy in nursery. It has to be worth my while to leave him there and go to work every day.

(Anna Capitanio, Vice-President, Organizational Effectiveness and M&A, BT Global Services)

A non-executive director also highlighted the importance of integrity:

Once you have retired and you are looking back you will ask yourself 'What do I have left?' Your career should be about *who* you were, not *what* you were. Very few people are allowed to retire with dignity these days, and once you are retired you have no corporate titles left. (Sheelagh Whittaker, Non-executive Director, Standard Life)

And with this emphasis on integrity, women need to find the right organization with the right culture:

You have the best chance of success if you are a genuine version of yourself. Be yourself. (Sheelagh Whittaker, Non-executive Director, Standard Life)

There is a business equivalent to 'you have to kiss a lot of frogs before you find your prince'. You need to find an organization where you fit in and where people will listen to your ideas. At my current company these people here are family. They have the same ideals as me. They are supporters of mine. (Monique Dumas, Investor Relations and Corporate Communications Partner, Electra Partners)

I could be myself – I swear like a trooper, never wear my shoes, and I collect Dennis the Menace ... the culture allowed me to be myself. I fitted in. (Senior manager, FTSE 100 company)

LESSONS LEARNED

Using leadership skills rather than technical knowledge

The biggest lesson for the interviewees to take away from working in a different environment was the confidence that they had a solid set of transferrable leadership skills that allowed them to work without having to rely on technical expertise. This enables them to demonstrate that they are leaders and business people rather than technical experts:

> I was not the expert but I understood the business and that was how I added value to the subject matter experts. I could not design programmes but I was good at managing the objectives and outputs. I want to know whether this works and what a good result would look like. My non-expert status forced me into that way of thinking and really allowed me to focus on business outcomes and ROI [return on investment]. (HR director, FTSE 100 company)

Another senior manager who talked about taking interim leadership roles in different functions pointed out:

> If you can run teams and run a P&L it doesn't matter what the genre is ... There is usually a team in place and you assess the team and work to their strengths. It is about getting people to speak in plain English. You help them see the wood for the trees ... I was looking at what people had to achieve and how we make it more efficient. I was asking myself 'Are people in the right roles?' ... I have worked in lots of areas where I was not an expert. It means that you are not locked into one sandpit ... I drew on past experience and asked questions: 'Why do we do it like this?' Breadth of experience is important if you want to be a manager. (Sophie Turner Laing, Managing Director, Entertainment and News, British Sky Broadcasting)

In addition to learning to draw on transferrable leadership skills, some of the interviewees also realized that they had skills they didn't think they had, such as being good at writing press releases despite not having a public relations background.

Flexibility

In addition to having transferrable leadership skills, another important lesson is adaptability and flexibility. Coming up against new ways of working allows people to adapt their own ways of working and makes them more flexible in their approach:

> Job roles are important as they show you where you have been. It is important that you get good foundations in your early jobs. I have

a broader role at Smith & Nephew with a smaller team than in some previous roles at larger organizations. A broad base early on is important as it gives you adaptability and flexibility, otherwise you get stuck and pigeonholed. (Susan Henderson, Company Secretary, Smith & Nephew)

As we saw in Chapter 5, learning to work in a different manner allows a woman to be more effective as she learns that there is more than one way of doing things and that her own style may not be effective in all situations. As the comment above shows, working in different environments does even more as it not only broadens a woman's working style but also her reputation. Without the diversity of having worked in different roles, organizations or industry sectors, a woman may become pigeonholed, which will limit her future career progression.

Learning from others

The interviewees talked about how they learned to adapt to their new work environment by asking others about approaches to certain situations, or by observing how others dealt with a person with whom they found it difficult to engage. Closely linked to the idea of learning from others is the use of allies, and the interviewees gave examples of how they found people early in their new roles who became trusted advisers. These people had often come from a background similar to that of the interviewee. These allies helped with decoding situations and highlighted what was and was not valued in the organization. They also gave advice on how to deal with difficult stakeholders. In addition to finding allies, building a trusted team that helps to deliver and is a source of learning is also vital. We heard in Chapter 7 about the importance of having a good team and will hear more about this in Chapter 9.

CAREER BENEFITS

Becoming a well-rounded leader

Developing strong transferrable leadership skills is not only one of the most important personal lessons of this critical job assignment, it is also valued by the organization and makes a woman a stronger contender for a senior role. Moving to a new area allows a woman to be seen more readily as a well-rounded leader who focuses on business issues rather than a specialist focusing on technical issues:

> I initially felt that my point of view wasn't valued but I learned that this was not the case. By being in meetings and by doing brainstorming it showed how I brought a unique country and hands-on operations view. I knew how things really worked day in, day out. My colleagues were often very theoretical and might miss things. They started to value my point of view and recognized my contributions. (Middle manager, FTSE 100 company)

> When I was promoted, I really benefited from this experience. It has made me more balanced and has allowed me to gain the respect of another team. It has allowed me to learn more about this part of the function, which meant that I could be more effective more quickly when I was promoted to oversee the entire area. I had gained a better understanding of the underlying risks. (Senior manager, property industry)

In addition to the career benefits of moving to a new environment in one's 'day job', numerous interviewees talked about the benefits of extracurricular activities, such as taking a leadership role in a charity or trade association, or joining a committee or task force in one's own organization. The main benefit women felt these roles had given them was the ability to demonstrate their leadership qualities in different arenas:

> Have outside interests and demonstrate leadership skills. For example, get involved in a trade organization. You need a track record of decision-making and living by decisions. (Claire Jenkins, Group Director Corporate Affairs, Rexam)

> All the extracurricular activities have more weight now that I am looking for non-executive director roles than the functional roles do as they are more strategy-focused, such as the senior manager promotion project or the global, cross-divisional project. They made me a rounded leader and gave me a broader profile internally. (Senior manager, FTSE 100 company)

Increased business acumen

The move to a new work environment also exposed the interviewees to new business models, cost pressures and markets, and therefore increased their business acumen, which further helped them to be regarded as well-rounded leaders;

> I moved to an adjacent industry and I learned about the wider context of the business. I also started to think about my skills in a transferrable context. (Jessica Burley, CEO, MCHI)

> It took me outside my silo. It gave me a broader perspective about the industry and the organization. I was more effective at senior management level when I talked about the organization. (Senior manager, FTSE 100 company)

Managers who move from operational roles to functional ones also often report gaining more understanding about corporate strategy and the corporate culture as a whole.[5]

Hitting the ground running

Another benefit of moving to a new function is being able to demonstrate that past achievements can be replicated in a new, unfamiliar territory. This gives a woman additional credibility and increases her leadership credentials. A senior manager in the finance industry talked about how she had been headhunted into a new role. She was told by the headhunter that her ability to move from one industry to another while still delivering outstanding results was an achievement that stood out. She had demonstrated she was able to get up to speed fast, a much sought after quality.

SUPPORT

Support for women comes from two main sources in the new work environment: managers and colleagues. Managers provide help with politics, opening doors and removing road blocks, as the following comment shows:

> I have the support from my boss and my boss's boss, who make sure that the right people hear me and that the right people are put

on my project. They help me open doors. My boss's boss has set up a meeting with the board so I can present my work. He has also lobbied board members before I presented: 'This is an important project, we need to support it.' He helped me create momentum. (Middle manager, FTSE 100 company)

But they also play a crucial role in helping to establish that all-important credibility so vital for women in these new situations: 'The CEO wanted my new role in the organization … he picked me out for praise in front of everyone else. He said that I had made the most fundamental change to the organization' (Senior manager, FTSE 100 company). For this assignment, more than for any of the others, the interviewees mentioned the importance of colleagues' support: 'Other people at work helped to open my eyes and set out where to expect resistance and what to expect of certain people. I try to get on with people in order to get help and support from others' (Middle manager, FTSE 100 company).

TIMING

Moving to a different role, industry or function is an experience that can happen at any time. The timing depends to some extent on what type of move it is. A move to a completely different *function* is easier if it happens earlier rather than later. As we saw in Chapter 6, moving from a functional area such as HR, legal or finance to an operational role becomes increasingly difficult the more senior a person gets. Similar thinking applies to moving to a different type of role within the same function – for example, when a woman moves from a research-focused role in marketing to a commercial role, though the time-frame during which this is possible is wider, as the woman remains in the same function. While a change of organization or industry sector early on will help to broaden a woman's working style and stop her from being pigeonholed, there may be other critical job assignments to look out for in those early days as these are much more difficult to undertake once children have arrived. Taking on an international assignment will have similar, and arguably more, benefits compared to changing industry sector or type of organization, and again is much harder to do once children have arrived. Moving to a new industry or organization, on the other hand, is easier to combine with child-care responsibilities. As a woman becomes more senior and becomes known for a particular skill such as turnaround, creating new business ventures or being a change agent, moving industries may be a good way of showing she is capable of delivering to exceptional levels, not just in familiar settings but also in completely new ones.

SUMMARY

New environments are good as they are stretching, and only if we are stretched do we learn. Moving to a different environment means a steep learning curve, and having to decode a new culture and new expectations, as well as establishing credibility and building new relationships – no small feat. However, the benefits of getting to grips with a different working environment are also significant. As one of the interviewees mentioned, 'not being locked in one sandpit' allows us to be flexible. The interviewees talked about improving their trans-ferrable skills, particularly leadership skills, as their technical skills were no longer very useful in the new role or the new work environ-ment. They also talked about becoming more flexible in their working styles and understanding the benefit of learning from others. Mov-ing to an unfamiliar environment helps a woman to build her career reputation in three important ways: it allows her to show that she is a well-rounded business leader rather than merely a technical expert; that she has good business acumen; and that she is capable of deliver-ing just as successfully in a new environment as before. Experiencing new work environments should happen throughout a woman's career; functional, and to some extent role moves, are easier earlier on, where-as industry and organizational moves can happen at any point and provide good confirmation of the transferrability of a woman's success in mid- and later career. The support that makes a difference during this assignment is again a manager's support, but this time also the support of colleagues. Managers provide support by giving a woman the opportunity to try a new role or even move to a new function. They also help her to decode her new environment. New colleagues also play an important part in this decoding process. In addition to the external challenges of the role, the interviewees talked about their internal journeys of self-discovery, which were explored in connec-tion with women-specific challenges. The In Focus section discussed the importance of finding the right organization and the right culture. A woman performs at her best where her values are in line with those of the organization and where she can be herself. In these situations women can maintain integrity, which is an important value for them.

TAKING ACTION

- **Broadening your base.** If you need to broaden your career experiences, then moving to a different role in your current organization or a different organization with a different business model may be a good opportunity to do so. What function, organization or industry would value the knowledge and skills you can bring from your current role? Moving from a more to a less sophisticated industry may allow you not only to make a level transfer but also to take a more senior role.
- **Building a track record.** If you already have a broad career base but need to develop your track record, then moving to a different industry will allow you to demonstrate that you are capable of achieving results no matter where you go.
- **Committee work.** If a move to a new role, organization or industry sector is not currently possible, you may benefit from joining a special task force or a committee at work to gain exposure to new business issues and test your leadership skills in a new context. This type of work will also allow you to build new relationships across your existing organization that will increase your visibility and can open doors to more interesting critical job assignments.

9

CREATING SOMETHING NEW: THE CORPORATE INTRAPRENEUR

Creating something new is important but successful women do that anyway. The business environment is male-oriented so women bring something new just by being there.
(Anna Capitanio, Vice-President, Organizational
Effectiveness and M&A HR, BT Global Services)

You can shape your own luck. You have to be brave. Jump off that cliff even if you are not 100 percent sure that there will be a safe landing. Be courageous and ask yourself what is the worst that can happen.
(Sophie Turner Laing, Managing Director, Entertainment
and News, British Sky Broadcasting)

Creating something new is a woman's opportunity to demonstrate her entrepreneurial spirit in a corporate setting. Innovation and renewal are important for organizations; without them, companies are rarely able to survive in today's fast-moving, competitive world. Innovation helps to deal with stagnant growth and the slowness of large, mature organizations.[1] Many large organizations are keen to bring entrepreneurial qualities in-house and embed these into their leadership definitions and competency frameworks. Others go even further and put their most promising managers through entrepreneurship training courses to increase ideas and the creation of new business ventures.[2] Corporate entrepreneurship is commonly referred to as 'intrapreneurship' and covers areas such as starting new business ventures and organizational renewal, where innovative insights create significant cost reductions and competitive advantages.[3] Neal Thornberry defines business ventures as 'The creation of something new that did not exist before. This 'something new' could be a new business-within-a-business, a product, a service, a delivery system, or a new value proposition to the customer' (p. 332).[4] Gifford Pinchot defines an intrapreneur as 'the dreamer who figures out how to turn an idea into a profitable reality' (p. ix). He therefore emphasizes the combination of identifying a business opportunity and the subsequent implementation of this venture.

Women entrepreneurs have been in the headlines for some time now. Various studies suggest that women leave large organizations to set up their own businesses as a way to escape the glass ceiling and to gain more flexibility.[5] The McKinsey study entitled *Women Matter*, however, also points to the importance of women bringing innovation to large, established companies.

A number of the interviewees in the study underpinning this book described themselves as innovative and creative, seeing these characteristics as their trade mark and as something that was valued by the organization. Creating something new is an area that women seem to fall into naturally and something that allows them to develop a leadership brand as they approach senior management. Together with change management and being a turnaround pro it is one of the three leadership skill sets that allow a woman to make her name and to stand out in her attempt to move to a senior leadership position. Creating something new is about creating a legacy and demonstrating you can make something stick. When the interviewees recalled their intrapreneurial assignments they talked about creating something that works, that improves the status quo, that delivers real value, and that is built in line with best practice. The challenges many of the interviewees relished were working with a blank piece of paper and creating something from nothing. The interviewees worked as intrapreneurs with a variety of remits. The majority of them were involved in setting up a new function or department, which involved developing a strategy, putting in place a team, aligning resources behind both, and delivering value for the business. But there are also other examples, such as creating a new business line, creating a value proposition for new products, or creating a tendering process for large-scale services. A small number of the interviewees talked about being pioneers in their area and being responsible for putting in place revolutionary processes, such as being among the first people to use a certain type of share exchange when acquiring a business, or being the first person in charge of developing a multi-channel retail solution.

Some of the activities listed above seem to require more intrapreneurial spirit than others. With most of the ventures listed, the interviewees were approached by the organization and asked to take on the challenge of setting up a new department or putting together a new value proposition. In these cases, the organization had already identified the need for change and innovation. Only in the cases where new product lines were suggested was it the woman herself who spotted the opportunity and proposed it to her senior management. It could be argued that these latter types of ventures are more intrapreneurial as they also include the initial stage of opportunity spotting in addition to realizing the opportunity. The numbers in this study are, however, too small to be able to draw any firm conclusions.

Let us look at how one senior manager described her experience of setting up a new business:

> This is the most daunting thing I have ever done. It was like having another child. It was truculent at times and divine at others. I had never written a business plan before, but there were always people around to help. You don't have to do it all yourself, you just need to know the right people to help you ... We were very lucky to take the team along. It was like we were all married; there was no need for a courting and honeymoon phase. We used shorthand and telepathy in the team ... We had to worry about the electricity bills, about paying everyone a salary, and setting up share structures, and we had to get the company funded. We were totally responsible for the business and the welfare of the team we had taken from the former company. I am not a financier. I can read a balance sheet but getting my head around that was difficult. (Sophie Turner Laing, Managing Director, Entertainment and News, British Sky Broadcasting)

Being entrepreneurial in a corporate setting is, of course, different than being a stand-alone entrepreneur who often risks his or her personal wealth and resources to build up a new venture. Within large organizations resources are available but often scarce, and the intrapreneur has to put forward a strong case as to why these resources should be made available to the new venture. New business-within-a-business ventures are also far from risk-free. In most cases there is no guarantee that the new venture will be successful and create the revenue or competitive advantage that is forecast. While an intrapreneur may not take the same financial risks as an entrepreneur, there will be a risk to her reputation or standing in the company. There are significant risks of failure from intrapreneurial activities but equally significant potential rewards for both the organization and the intrapreneur. In his Intrapreneur's Ten Commandments, Pinchot points to a variety of different challenges intrapreneurs have to deal with, including taking risks to one's job security by working on a risky venture; overcoming multiple and varied organizational obstacles; and being ready to deal with what he calls the 'corporate immune mechanism', which will attack any new idea or venture as soon as it surfaces. There is also the need to build the right team and understand the importance of finding and working closely with sponsors. As we shall see below, the interviewees' own experiences echo a number of these challenges.

JOB-SPECIFIC CHALLENGES

Devising a strategy and business plan

Building something new requires a vision of what the new function, product or process will look like, and more important, what it will do for the organization. Pinchot points out that 'intrapreneurs ride to the discovery of successful ventures on the strength of their vision' (p. 37).[6] It is this vision that has to be transformed into an effective strategy, and then into an inspiring business plan, to obtain much needed buy-in and access to often scarce organizational resources. An intrapreneur's business plan has to cover a diverse range of areas including cash flow projections, marketing propositions, staffing plans and operational considerations. Thornberry reported that, when they worked with a number of large organizations on business planning for intrapreneurs, the business planning skills required for intrapreneurial activities often overwhelmed the managers' current skills level in business planning. A business plan is also an important recruitment and pre-selling tool. It helps the intrapreneur to share her ideas with others in an effort to secure their support.[7] As conversations take place and the business plan matures, opinions about the new venture are being formed within the organization. By the time the business plan is ready it has almost become obsolete as by then the decision whether to proceed with the proposed venture or not will often have already been taken.[8] The business planning process therefore has to be closely linked to ongoing conversations, opinion-canvassing and the building of a support base. A number of the interviewees talked about how they had to pull together business plans and then pitch for a budget, often large amounts of money, to fund their proposed business ventures. When they talked about presenting their business cases, they mentioned how presenting their plans to senior management, and in many cases the board, gave them good visibility in the organization. It is a powerful combination: high visibility, talking about business ventures that have a direct impact on the bottom line, and putting forward arguments strong enough to help secure substantial amounts of money. As we shall see later, the career benefits resulting from successful intrapreneurial activities are substantial.

Building a support base

Support for the new business idea has to be garnered across the organization. The following comment illustrates this well:

> I set up the role and created the function. I had no trust or credibility. I had to prove myself and work hard. I had to deliver results and have a plan and communicate that plan. You need sponsors and to get people on board in small chunks. Find new champions every day. You have to demonstrate tenacity and confidence and get people on board. (Paola Cuneo, General Manager, BT)

One interviewee pointed out that there are always people in an organization who can support you, but these people have to be found first. Building a support base also requires a woman to draw heavily on her influencing and persuasion skills:

> I had to get consensus across countries and engage the directors and take them along. The challenge was the complexity of getting lots of people involved and getting decisions made without compromising. (Anja Madsen, Operations Development Manager, Tesco)

> My career to date had been about making improvements but now it was about creating something new. In the past it was about 'How do I get from A to B?' But now there was no B. The biggest challenge was persuasion. (Senior executive, FTSE 100 company)

Supporters come in many different shapes and forms, and senior supporters are particularly important. Pinchot calls supporters 'the protectors of ideas' (p. 143). They provide political cover while the intrapreneur focuses on dealing with the daily challenges of realizing her new business venture. Sponsors also help to secure resources. Ideally, sponsors should be brave, and not afraid of controversy, be supporters of new ideas generally, be politically astute, and respected by other senior decision-makers.[9]

Establishing credibility

Credibility is key to career success in so many different situations, and it plays a particularly important role with intrapreneurial activities. A new idea, the need for scarce organizational resources, no guarantee that the new venture will work – without the intrapreneur's credibility no new business venture will get very far. The following quotes illustrate very effectively how women have to work hard to build credibility. The quotes refer to a communications partner's experience of repeatedly setting up new public relations and communications functions for organizations where there previously had been none. In this first quote she talks about the challenges of establishing her own credibility:

> Throughout my career most of my roles were start-up roles. I always started with nothing. When I'd come in as a younger woman and tell people that they had the wrong idea about marketing and communications, they used to react with 'Bless, she is trying' but wouldn't take me seriously. The best way to deal with that was to be present at all meetings so that I visually became part of the team. I absorbed everything. I was thinking outside the box and was presenting my ideas to my boss. At the start he would say 'No, I don't think so'. Eventually he would say, 'Yes, that is a good idea'. You have to get one person on your side. You have to be seen as being essential. My boss would then involve me in meetings and get me to present my idea. He would say 'Monique had this great idea. Actually, Monique, why don't you tell them about it?' (Monique Dumas, Investor Relations and Corporate Communications Partner, Electra Partners)

She then went on to talk about the additional challenges of establishing credibility for her function; the challenges of demonstrating that what she is proposing will add real business value:

> PR is not seen as important, not seen as being responsible for the bottom line. You have to be heard and be seen to have something

useful to add. It is often, 'The PR girl, it's all fluff.' You face resistance and you have to do twice as much, as they are not willing to cooperate. If you ask them to write a press release they will not do it. The only way I could get them to contribute was to draft the release for them and ask for comments. Only then would they say 'That's not right, this is what it should say', and mark up my draft. You need confidence and assertiveness, and to demonstrate the impact of your actions. They need to see you as part of their team. (Monique Dumas, Investor Relations and Corporate Communications Partner, Electra Partners)

While building credibility and trust is vital for the success of intrapreneurial activities, Antoncic and colleagues also talk about the importance of being trusting oneself, as this will help to build partnerships with many different stakeholders in an organization.[10]

Dealing with resistance, bureaucracy and infrastructure constraints

Even after support has been gained from various stakeholders, the interviewees talked about a variety of additional challenges they encountered when it came to realizing their ideas. People's resistance and organizational infrastructure hurdles are the biggest problems. Responses such as 'This cannot be done', 'The organization is not set up to realize this vision', and 'We do not have the right supplier base for this' were frequently encountered by the interviewees. A few middle management interviewees also talked about the frustrations of large organizations being slow and inert. Some of these women had come from consulting backgrounds and may have found the challenges of getting things done in a large organization particularly testing. Resistance to change and organizational red tape are two common reasons for intrapreneurial activities to fail. Other reasons often mentioned are a lack of resources, a lack of support and a lack of appropriate recognition for the reputational risks taken by the employee.[11] While it may be easy to assume that large organizations struggle with the generation of ideas, but are effective at implementing and realizing these once they have been generated, it has been pointed out that the opposite is true: ideas aplenty are generated but they often fail at the implementation stage. Pinchot talks about an implementation crisis.[12] But it is this final hurdle of actual implementation that separates the successful from the unsuccessful intrapreneur. Where intrapreneurs are hitting barriers and obstacles they have to go around these, often by doing something themselves rather than asking others in the organization to do it for them. The reason intrapreneurs often encounter obstacles is that at the start nobody understands the intrapreneur's proposed venture well enough to see how it can be implemented.[13] One interviewee, for example, talked about how she had to sit down with the organization's supply chain team to build a supply chain that would allow her to source the new product she was developing for the organization.

Building the right team

While an intrapreneur may have to do a lot of work herself, she will be unlikely to be successful without having the right team in place. We saw in Chapter 7 just how important building and managing teams is to a woman's success in delivering against her objectives time and again. Setting up a new business venture, be it a new department, product or value proposition, is a formidable task and can rarely be achieved alone. It is important to find people who are willing to work on a venture where success is not guaranteed. In this context, it is not only the intrapreneur's ability to *build* a new team that challenges her leadership skills but also the *manner* in which she has to lead that team. Intrapreneurs have to be decisive leaders, able to give clear direction in times of uncertainty, instill belief in the cause, and take decisions when little data is available. Intrapreneurs also have to tackle the additional hurdle of starting from a position of no power, when they yet have to prove themselves and their business idea a success. Therefore, they need strong personal leadership, vision and inspiration to motivate others to follow them.[14]

WOMEN-SPECIFIC CHALLENGES

Serving the tea

The interviewees talked at length about dealing with men's expectations and the additional problems this created for them. The examples are very varied and range from being expected to serve the tea in meetings to behaving in a warm and nurturing way. They also include men's preconceptions about what additional responsibilities a mother may be able or willing to take on. The following comments illustrate these points:

> I never had to say 'no' because of my children as I have an extended support network … a nanny, my husband helps out, a childminder, my parents and parents-in-law, but sometimes people who know that I have children make decisions without consulting me. I went to an interview recently and could see the surprise in the interviewers' eyes when I mentioned that I had children. (Paola Cuneo, General Manager, BT)

> I received some negative feedback from my senior managers that I come across as a bit cold but they struggled to quantify what they expected. It was a very aggressive and temperamental culture which is not like me. I discussed this feedback with my partner, who suggested that they expect every woman to be friendly and warm and may not be used to women standing their ground. I was also the only woman, so they had nobody to compare me to. It comes back to confidence. If you are not that confident, you are less relaxed and as a result spend less time on chit-chat. Generally though I am more business-like and analytical. (Senior manager, FTSE100 organization)

> There were senior PR people, clients, lawyers … and they thought that I was there to serve the tea. They didn't give me their business cards and I saw people's surprise when I contributed to the meeting. I got used to it, but it took a while for me to swallow it. I was judged before I opened my mouth … The tea thing will always stay with me. It is a key piece of grounding for me. It is my measuring stick. (Monique Dumas, Investor Relations and Corporate Communications Partner, Electra Partners)

A number of the interviewees recounted experiences similar to the last comment here. Most of the interviewees initially rebelled against the expectation that they will serve tea and coffee. They were still trying to establish their credibility and working out how to deal with these situations. Interestingly, as the interviewees became more senior and with unquestionable track records behind them, some are now strategically using the serving of tea and coffee as a way of having one-to-one conversations with someone during a large meeting, or as a way to collect 'brownie points' to be redeemed later.

LESSONS LEARNED

Listening to the women during the interviews, there were two lessons they took from this type of assignment more than any other – confidence and stakeholder management.

If I can do this, I can do anything

Confidence boosters are important for everyone. A career journey is rarely smooth and often blocked by obstacles. All the assignments discussed in this book provided a critical confidence-boosting moment for one or other interviewee. Interestingly, though, when I evaluated the learning that the interviewees had taken from creating something new, confidence-building emerged much more frequently from this critical job assignment than from any other assignment. Here is what some of the women had to say:

> This role allowed me to bring out my unique skills set: creative and analytical skills. I can fluctuate effectively between the big picture and detail. The role gave me a personal confidence boost that this is unique about me. The role played to my strengths and brought out the total me that other roles couldn't. (Senior manager, FTSE 100 company)

> This project gave me self-confirmation that being myself is good enough. (Senior manager, FTSE 100 company)

A boost in confidence is an important benefit gained from the experience of creating something new, but intrapreneurs have to be equipped with a fair amount of confidence to start with. The risks of the new venture failing are real, and the obstacles to implementing one's idea are significant. Without a good dose of self-confidence, the intrapreneur would not be able to realize her vision of a new business venture.[15]

IN FOCUS: SELF-CONFIDENCE

One of the themes that emerged in virtually every interview is self-confidence. It plays a big part in how well we perform; if we believe in ourselves we are more likely to persist and succeed. But even the most confident of us occasionally suffer crises of confidence and it is our external environment that can either destroy or boost our confidence. Almost every woman talked about at least one situation in which a new role was a big step up and brought with it some self-doubt: 'Can I do this job?' The interviewees tended to overcome these doubts by working incredibly hard and by getting encouragement from significant others in their lives, such as bosses, mentors and sponsors, friends and often partners. Some of the most important confidence-builders are supportive bosses. They believe in a woman, are willing to take risks by allowing her to take on new challenges in areas where she might not yet have proved herself, and readily tell other senior colleagues of her achievements and recommend her for projects. Another important source of confidence is a woman's partner. His belief in her makes a tremendous difference. In addition to helping out with childcare arrangements, the type of partner support that most interviewees talked about was knowing that their partners had utter faith in their abilities. Another effective confidence-booster is mastering a difficult assignment to great acclaim. It shows a woman her capabilities. The concept of self-belief is so central that when I asked the senior women about the best career advice they had received, most of them talked about someone telling them they could do it, that they are good, and that they can go as far as they want to.

Stakeholder management

Stakeholders are people who have to be included in decision-making as they either influence the final outcome of a decision or are affected by it. To ensure that decisions are well-received, involving both those influencing and those being affected by decisions at an early stage is important. The interviewees talked about learning who their key stakeholders are and who can be left out of stakeholder management activities, as the following comments show:

> The more senior you are the less it is about delivering and the more it is about getting stakeholders on board. (Senior manager, FTSE 100 company)

> Initially I got too many people involved and learned that I had to work with the key opinion formers whom the other directors would follow. While it is good to create consensus there are more efficient ways of doing things: working with fewer people, moving

forward and showing the others later. (Middle manager, FTSE 100 company)

One interviewee also talked about the importance of 'thinking big' with regard to stakeholder management. She talked about going beyond typical stakeholder groups and exploring what value can be gained from including less immediately obvious stakeholders. She pointed out that while she had spent a lot of time involving internal stakeholders she realized too late that she should have involved an external stakeholder group which had a significant, if indirect, impact on the value proposition she was creating.

Influencing others

Influencing skills are universally important and a part of daily corporate life. They also apply to many of the other critical job assignments. The reason presentation skills have been introduced here is that creating something new involves a significant amount of presenting business cases, pitching for resources and generally putting forward arguments in favour of the proposed venture. A key element of influencing others effectively is to tailor one's message to the audience, as the following comments show:

I had to persuade the operations director and do lots of selling in. The operations director was different from the finance directors I had worked with before. I used different skills and arguments to get through to him, and learned to adapt how I communicated. (Senior manager, FTSE 100 company)

It was a large territory and a different culture. It was difficult to drive the agenda through many different countries. You need to switch messages and switch them fast, learn about different styles, adapt your own approach and understand others' agendas. You have to be consistent and have your own plan; eventually you will get it through. (Paola Cuneo, General Manager, BT)

CAREER BENEFITS

While the risks to one's reputation from intrapreneurial ventures are potentially large, the potential rewards are equally big. One of the career benefits of being an intrapreneur is the ability to show beyond doubt one's capability to succeed in uncertain and complex situations.

Demonstrating your capabilities and creating a legacy

For many of the other critical job assignments, the interviewees talked about how they had demonstrated personal qualities, such as well-rounded leadership and increased business acumen. For this assignment more than any of the others, they emphasized the final deliverable as a way of showing bosses and colleagues what they had achieved:

'I demonstrated that I could meet their needs. I provided them with a function and a service they didn't expect they could get' (Senior manager, FTSE 100 company).

The interviewees seemed to be particularly proud of creating a legacy. They talked about being able to set up something from nothing and it becoming fully afloat. A number of them also talked about building something to best practice standards that provided the foundations for future development and in many cases was still in place despite the women having moved on. This is how one of the interviewees described it:

It is about creating something new. In the world we are in, and also where we are headed, this is important. You have to be able to show that you can build the next thing. Nothing is stable and that will be the case even more so in the next 20 years. You have to be able to innovate. This experience built my confidence that I can resolve problems and create something that sticks around for longer. (Anna Capitanio, Vice-President, Organizational Effectiveness and M&A, BT Global Services)

Now I am visible

In Chapter 3 the importance of becoming visible in an organization was considered at length. With the recognition of a job well done and a clear legacy to refer back to, this much-needed visibility becomes a reality:

I was working in an area that was new to the organization. I developed the offering and found funding for it. As it was a new area I was more visible than I would have usually been. (Senior manager, FTSE 100 company)

An acclaimed business writer declared this business start-up the outstanding business achievement of the year. (Sheelagh Whittaker, Non-executive Director, Standard Life)

Becoming widely known outside one's organization as a way to further cement personal credibility was mentioned by a number of the interviewees. Creating a legacy gave them interesting material for talks at industry events, newspaper interviews and articles in trade journals. Elin Hurvenes, founder of the Professional Boards Forum, advises women to build an online presence: 'If all that comes up in a Google search about your name is your Facebook site, then that is not good news.'[16]

SUPPORT

Line manager support is again important for this critical job assignment. Managers can help to remove barriers but they are also important in helping a woman to 'see the wood for the trees'. They help to provide a reality check and to make sure problems are kept in perspective. The most effective managers during this type of job assignment are those who truly value innovation and intrapreneurial activities. Just as a new business venture is risky for the intrapreneur herself, her manager is also taking a risk. Managers can support intrapreneurs by applying a different time horizon when it comes to judging success and performance, as intrapreneurial activities often take longer to come to fruition.[17] Wider organizational support is, however, also crucial. As we saw earlier, women need to draw on the skills of sponsors and other supporters to help them convince a large number of stakeholders that their business venture ideas are worth progressing.

In a much broader sense, support for intrapreneurs starts early. In a study of intrapreneurs, (all interviewees were male, as in sufficient numbers of female intrapreneurs could be found), Cox and Jennings[18] found that almost all of the intrapreneurs in their sample reported that they had experienced challenging assignments early in their careers, and they had to learn to deal with problems without the support of others. This finding provides further evidence for the importance of early stretch assignments, as was seen in Chapter 4. These early learning opportunities, made possible by supportive bosses, allow a woman to build the necessary resilience and resourcefulness to tackle large-scale challenges, such as building new business ventures later in her career.

TIMING

It is never too early for a woman to try her hand at innovation and putting in place new ideas. However, there seemed to be agreement among the interviewees that, to start a new business venture, a woman needs to have a number of years of prior experience. The interviewees agreed that only with a certain amount of knowledge and experience behind them were they able to build the credibility that was necessary for this type of job assignment. One interviewee, who had built a career from setting up functions in new organizations, talked about the importance of having experience across the entire range of her function and of having the necessary relationships. She said:

> You need a clear understanding of how to do it. You need to understand the basics. If you build a house with only three cornerstones, then when the wind blows it will fall apart. You mustn't forget anything. You also need to have sponsors who can help you and lobby for you. (Monique Dumas, Investor Relations and Corporate Communications Partner, Electra Partners)

The interviewees seemed largely to agree that, in order to be a successful intrapreneur, this critical job assignment is best tackled from middle management level onwards.

SUMMARY

Creating something new is one of the three potential 'making-your-name' assignments that allow a woman to become widely known as a leader. Intrapreneurial activities are valued by organizations, as successful business-within-business ventures can make the difference between continued and stagnant growth. Successful intrapreneurs are good at both spotting business opportunities and at implementing them effectively. To do this well, women have to develop strategies, build a support base and overcome an organization's bureaucracy and infrastructure constraints. Women-specific challenges are centered around overcoming stereotypical expectations, such as serving the tea in meetings. While the challenges of creating something new are significant, so are the lessons that the interviewees took from this experience. 'If I can do this, I can do anything' was a reaffirmation of their capability that many of the interviewees took from this experience. Stakeholder management and influencing are other lessons that the assignment provided. Creating a legacy and demonstrating the ability to set up a new business venture are powerful career accelerators and provide increased visibility for the women. Risk-embracing and innovative managers who help a woman to focus her priorities provide the best support. Equally important, though, are sponsors who help to protect the business idea and help to secure buy-in. Innovation is a good experience to have early in one's career, but the interviewees agreed that in order to be able to have enough support networks, access to the right people and generally enough business experience, large-scale intrapreneurial ventures are best left to the middle management phase and beyond.

TAKING ACTION

- **Are you an intrapreneur?** Do you relish taking commercial risks and proving to others that you can achieve results where others do not dare to go? Establish what type of intrapreneurial activity works best for you. Ask yourself if you are motivated by spotting innovative business ideas, such as new product lines or new service provisions, or do you prefer implementing innovative ideas that have already been approved at the highest level in the organization, such as building a new HR function at head office or a new sales function abroad?
- **Intrapreneurial qualities**. Assess your own skills set and your intrapreneurial reputation. What can you learn from highly-regarded intrapreneurs in your organization? What are your current strengths, and where do you have to develop further? Identify a colleague or boss who is particularly good at building business cases or managing stakeholders and learn by observing his/her actions.

- **Getting the right assignment.** Mention your desire to work on an intrapreneurial project to your boss and sponsor. Surround yourself with people known in the organization for innovation; you will be more likely to learn about future intrapreneurial ventures and increase your chances of getting involved in these.

10

MERGING, DOWNSIZING AND REENGINEERING: THE CHANGE AGENT

Put it all into context. Don't allow yourself to be overwhelmed by current problems. What would your future self say and do now?
(Jo Pisani, Partner, PricewaterhouseCoopers)

Successful women are known for one thing that they have done exceptionally well. What are you known for that follows you around? What is your brand?
(Senior Manager, FTSE 100 Company)

Organizational change is a fact of corporate life. Organizations have to adapt continually to new markets, competition and other external factors. Barely a day goes by when we do not hear of a high-profile merger, downsizing decisions or other business process re-engineering programs. As change is a major element of corporate life, having proved oneself to be an effective change agent is an important tick in the box on the way to the top. Kotter uses organizational change as a differentiator between managers and leaders.[1] Managers deal with organizational complexity, whereas leaders prepare organizations for change and help them to deal with it. Organizational change is a summary term that includes different types of transformations an organization may undergo in response to internal and external pressures. The examples the interviewees described map broadly on to the three levels of organizational change described by Lawson and Price.[2] The first level of changes they describe are changes involving direct actions, such as divesting certain parts of the company in order to focus on core elements. This type of change does not require employees to change the way they work. But it has a profound impact on those who work in the parts of the company that are about to be stripped away. One interviewee, for example, described how she led the integration process after the purchase of a new business. Her role during this integration was to close down one of the operations units. While there was limited impact from this initiative on the wider organization, the effect on the site that was being closed down was significant. The interviewee's challenges centered around closing down the site while maintaining the dignity and self-esteem of the employees affected. At the next level of change, employees need to adopt new behaviors or adapt existing ones, but these are still in line with their current values and mindset. An example here is a company that already operates a lean business model and asks employees to look for ways of becoming even leaner. A number of the interviewees talked about how they had been asked to run cost-cutting programs to help identify further cost savings in an organization that was already known for its streamlined operations. Finally, the deepest and most complex level of change is one that requires a change in the employees' mindset, something typically referred to as cultural change. A number of the interviewees talked about how they had been put in charge of significantly updating a department or global processes.

Let us look at two examples of interviewees' experiences of taking on an organizational change assignment:

I got a tip-off from someone that they were looking to rebuild the management team out there with more English speakers. I applied for the role. They valued my flexibility, my understanding of the nitty-gritty of operations and my MBA. I had lots of advocates in the corporate center and a strong support base … I had very rusty French and it was a hairy assignment. I had to turn a cosmetics factory into one producing pharmaceuticals. We needed not only radical process changes but also a culture change. I was always on tenterhooks as to what the gung-ho team was about to do. I had to break strikes, had to deal with a drunken workforce. But I enjoyed the buzz and the diversity. (Jo Pisani, Partner, PricewaterhouseCoopers)

I had to quickly formulate a vision and strategy and give confidence to the board. I had to present a well-thought-through plan, understand the issue and agree a route forward. The size of the challenge was 10,000 people in customer service. I had to get to the people at the front line. I had to work out how to listen without disempowering middle managers. I helped people to see their purpose: 'We need to help customers in times of need.' I also had to implement [my changes] quickly throughout the organization in an inspirational manner. (Senior manager, finance industry)

Change initiatives are fraught with potential pitfalls, and few mergers and acquisitions produce the synergy effects and cost savings originally envisaged. A McKinsey global survey of successful transitions found that, to be successful, change efforts had to have clear and aspirational goals, and to galvanize and maintain buy-in throughout the organization. Strong leadership is also required.[3]

JOB-SPECIFIC CHALLENGES

The human element: dealing with emotions

Dealing with emotions is the challenge that interviewees talked about more than any other. They encountered different types of emotions, such as shock, anger and a fear of change, which led to resistance and to the outright blocking of ideas. While emotions do not fall into neat categories, the types of emotions encountered by the interviewees seem to map broadly on to the three levels of change set out by Lawson and Price, which provide a useful way of organizing the data. While divesting the company of business assets, an example of a Level 1 change, does not affect organization-wide values, it has a pronounced impact on the part of the business that is being sold off. Many of the interviewees talked about having to make difficult downsizing decisions: closing offices and operations, and making staff redundant. These are complex and emotionally-charged situations, and making people redundant is an experience that many interviewees said had stayed with them. The interviewees talked about having to deal with the shock and anger of others, and learning to deal with these emotions with empathy and tact: 'It was a very difficult time and I had to show others that the organization was not that well run. I spent nine months taking people through the changes and I had to maintain their self- esteem' (HR Director, FTSE 100 company).

With a Level 2 change, where a woman has to persuade people to adapt their existing behaviors in order to achieve outcomes such as cost savings, the emotion the interviewees talked about facing most often was the fear of 'looking bad' in cost analysis calculations which led to resistance:

I was in a change management role. I faced resistance from stakeholders due to my cost cutting remit. They were afraid of being the 'bad person'. I had to win people over, which took time, but at the same time I had to keep up the momentum. (Middle manager, FTSE 100 company)

148

Long-standing talent was set in its ways and I had to help people to change and move on. There was a lot of dialogue to get them on side. (CEO, UK company)

It is particularly difficult to deal with organizational change that threatens existing functions and leaders. One woman talked about the vested interests she encountered, and how people resisted her work as they feared that their function would be highlighted as being less efficient: 'There were lots of vested interests and I had to work across functions. I faced resistance 'This hasn't been done before', 'I am not coming out looking good from your analysis; something must be wrong' (Senior manager, telecommunications industry).

With a Level 3 change, where new values and attitudes are required, the interviewees reported not only facing resistance but also out-right blocking of their vision and plans. One interviewee, for example, talked about the challenge of building an IT system to support a new HR function. She was told by the organization's IT department that what she wanted to do was not possible. To help her realize her vision, she hired a team of external IT people to help her develop the system that she needed. Barbara Senior's list of individual driving forces against change includes fears of the unknown, a potential loss of one's power base or one's rewards, and concerns that one's current skills will no longer be valued in the new situation and or that they may not be sufficient to deal effectively with the new role.[4] All these fears are likely to surface during fundamental cultural change projects. Lee and King recommend emphasizing the continuity of values, goals and identity wherever possible during a change initiative.[5] Being able to build on existing values makes it easier for people to take action in the face of uncertainty. Research into organizational change initiatives has shown that the human element is one of the most important factors in determining success, and one that is all too often overlooked.[6]

Dealing with a lack of information and knowledge

Another challenge the interviewees faced during their organizational change assignments was missing information. Information is important to enable a change leader to understand the organization's status quo, its ability to deal with the forthcoming changes, and the extent to which mindsets will have to change.[7] Without a thorough initial assessment, a change leader's efforts may be misguided. In some cases, the interviewees were also new to an area, lacked important knowledge and had to become experts in a short time. Nevertheless, they recognized the need to take action:

> I had a double role of finance director and being responsible for the integration. It was a completely new area for me and I had to close down offices with dignity. It was a complex situation. I was not always prepared for things but still had to talk with integrity about them. (Senior manager, FTSE 100 company)

> Some of the areas I took on were very complex. I had to work out how to influence and lead while not knowing everything. (CEO, UK company)

One interviewee talked about how it was difficult to find the right information, and how she had to work her way through many different types of information to discover the right facts and figures. When another interviewee did not have the right experience to run a change project, she was told she had simply to get the right people into her team to deal with the technical issues. Yet another interviee remarked on the need to take risks:

> You have to take risks to do something new. You constantly have to encourage change as you are always fighting market share. It is difficult to be certain during change but you need to take small, iterative steps rather than exploring and considering too much. I have been involved in cost management, restructure, redundancies, getting a long-term view of costs. (Jessica Burley, CEO of MCHI)

WOMEN-SPECIFIC CHALLENGES

Dealing with male chauvinism and paternalistic thinking

The following comments illustrate the chauvinism and paternalistic thinking the interviewees had to deal with:

> There were lots of male managers at the regional meetings. They would say 'Here comes the bird from head office.' I had to push through resistance and male chauvinism. I had to get in there and

fight my corner. They learned that I wasn't going to be pushed around. (Senior manager, FTSE 100 company)

A senior manager who was in an international role and expecting a child recalled:

It was a very male-dominated and intimidating environment. I worked with a lot of men who didn't see women as belonging in senior management, particularly when they are pregnant. I heard some very paternalistic comments, such as 'You should be look-ing for a cushy job in head office and get flexible working times.' (Senior manager, FTSE 100 company)

A similar experience was described in Chapter 5, in the context of combining global roles with childcare responsibilities.

Another senior manager recalled her experiences:

In this environment there was no discussion about balance and it was disrespectful towards women. It was male and chauvinistic. The language with which senior managers talk about women was disrespectful, such as 'She is dizzy', 'She is an airhead'. I tried to challenge [this] in a respectful manner but was told after the meet-ing that I was uptight. (Senior manager, FTSE 100 company)

LESSONS LEARNED

Helping others to deal with change

When the interviewees talked about helping others to deal with change, they emphasized the importance of recognizing and accept-ing others' emotions and reactions, and of working with these emo-tions rather than against them. Interestingly, this applies to both a woman's reports and her managers:

When you take people through the cycle of change, don't fight their emotions. Let them go through it and help them work it out. Recog-nize that everyone is different. (Senior manager, finance industry)

It was a very hierarchical organization and many senior managers were not approachable. When I had to present unfavourable news to senior managers they were not prepared to have a discussion. They regarded their opinion as the right one. I had to try not to be confrontational as I would have never won a fight. I learned to discuss tricky issues bit by bit and to avoid bad surprises. It was important to win allies in their teams and I had to find someone at their level who supported my ideas and use these people to make my point. (Middle manager, FTSE 100 company)

Another important element of helping others deal with their emotions during times of change is ongoing communication. Organizational change creates uncertainty and upheaval, and communication is an important tool to help those affected by change to deal with the situation more easily. Ongoing communication can allay people's fears and effective change agents communicate frequently even when there is nothing new to pass on. As we saw earlier in this chapter, emotions loom large at times of organizational change. This means that the interviewees had to learn to do more than simply to communicate clearly. They had to learn to make their messages appeal at an emotional level.[8] Creating a compelling story is an important ingredient to galvanizing energies behind a change effort. Aiken and Keller warn, however, that a story which motivates senior managers may not necessarily motivate all the important stakeholders in the organization.[9] Therefore a leader has to adapt her communication carefully to make sure she can secure as much buy-in to her plans as possible. Interestingly, one interviewee also talked about how she helped her team to move to a performance-driven culture by focusing on their communication and persuasion skills: 'I learned that when you move from a process-driven culture to a performance-driven culture you have to give others the tools to do their jobs effectively, such as presentation skills, influencing and building business cases' (Senior manager, finance industry).

Learning from senior stakeholders

Organizational change contains a strong political element as it often shifts lines of power in an established organization.[10] While stakeholder management is routinely listed as one of the main difficulties during organizational change projects, the interviewees did not mention it as a challenge. They did, however, talk about how working with senior managers during times of organizational change helped them to gain vital insights into the ways that the organization's leaders work and think, and what they value:

I learned a lot from senior stakeholders; for example, what is important and what is not, how they interact with each other and how they change their style when they interact with others. I got an understanding of who they are and saw them up close. I saw that they are good but that it's not impossible to act at their level. It was a real confidence booster. (Senior manager, FTSE 100 company)

I learned a lot from this project. The exposure to very senior people gave me security. You need to go prepared but they are humans too. It gave me practice in [ways of] convincing them. Initially, the senior managers didn't respect my background. I had to try to win them over. While I hadn't managed [this area] before, I was willing to work there and to bring the senior team the numbers to support my recommendations. My main stakeholders had to be won over and I had to prove that I can add value. I had to try and think like them and try to understand what concerns them. I had to put myself into their shoes, and understand their fears and address them. (Middle manager, FTSE 100 company)

We heard in Chapter 4 about the importance of gaining a senior management perspective as part of an early stretch assignment. Working with senior stakeholders during times of change allows a woman to build on this earlier experience and get an even better insight into how senior managers work and think, particularly in times of uncertainty.

CAREER BENEFITS

Being seen as a change agent

No organization can afford to stand still, and reinvention, adaptation and prompt reaction to external events are vital to organizational survival. Being able to convince an organization of the need for change, being capable of creating a vision and bringing people along with you, and making new values and processes stick are important skills that require determination, great persuasion and stakeholder management skills. These are much-valued skills and allow a woman to make her name. The emphasis for change agents is very much on delivering results, as the following two comments illustrate well:

> Organizational change is important for certain roles; for example, an operations director. You think of these people as more experienced if they have gone through it. (HR director, FTSE 100 company)

> Sorting out existing problems and instigating change is really important, more and more so now. You have to be known for delivery; for example, divesting part of a business or cutting costs. (Senior manager, finance industry)

IN FOCUS: MAKING YOUR NAME

There seem to be one or two assignments among all the critical job assignments that a woman is likely to come across on her way to the top that are real game changers. The stakes for these assignments are ultra high and so is the level of visibility. These assignments allow a woman to cement her reputation and make her name in her company and beyond. These projects and achievements are what a woman will be known for:

> Successful women are known for one thing that they have done exceptionally well; for example, cost saving or turnaround. You have to demonstrate to the organization that you are making a real difference and that you can deliver. You have to ask yourself what you are known for that follows you around. (Senior manager, FTSE 100 company)

These assignments allow a woman to break through the glass ceiling and join the senior management ranks. By the time these assignments come along, a woman will have already delivered a number of highly regarded projects and built a track record. Many of the interviewees talked about these assignments drawing everything together that they had learned up to that date. It's the one assignment that brings out the true person with all her unique capabilities – her signature strengths:

> The role allowed me to bring out my unique skills set: creative and analytical skills; fluctuating between the big picture and

---

154

the detail. It gave me a personal confidence boost that this is unique about me. The role played to my strengths and brought out the total picture [where] other roles couldn't. This role gave me external recognition for a job well done. (Senior manager, FTSE 100 company)

These assignments separate a woman from the rest. One senior manager recalled the time when she was interviewed to join the executive committee of her organization: 'When I was interviewed for this role they told me 'You are tried and tested. Your record stands before you'' (Senior manager, FTSE 100 company).

This is the role that makes the organization as a whole, and often the industry the woman is operating in, sit up and take notice. Examples of such roles are quite diverse, ranging from a company takeover which was the biggest deal of its kind, involving a wide range of complicated processes, to holding one of the biggest budgets in the country, having a team of hundreds of people with many opportunities for the role to go wrong. With these assignments the hours are usually long, the scrutiny through the board is high, and the expected deliverables are tough. But these roles allowed the interviewees to hone their 'all-round' skills sets, ranging from presentation skills and stakeholder management to general business acumen. At the same time, they also provided another confidence boost, which encouraged the interviewees to trust their instincts and to feel confident and in control. These assignments are important stepping stones to the most senior roles in the organization which will be discussed in Chapter 12. They are grand slam assignments and do not come along very often.

Seeing the organization more holistically

Seeing the organization more holistically and joining up the dots are important lessons valued by companies and their senior management. It allows a leader to be more effective in her delivery of results. The types of organizational change explored in this chapter were mainly large-scale initiatives that allowed the interviewees to understand how different parts of an organization fit together and impact on each other. One interviewee, for example, talked about learning how the various processes she had been asked to update worked across the global operations of the organization. She learned to see them in their entirety. The following comments make similar points:

> Running organizational change is like creating something new, and women are successful at this. It gives you the big picture and an understanding of how all is changing. You are connecting the dots. (Anna Capitanio, Vice-President, Organizational Effectiveness and M&A HR, BT Global Services)

> I demonstrated that I understood the importance of relationship building and I gained a better insight into how the business works. I made the connections and understood the impact my actions had on various parts of the business, such as branding, sales, back office operations and IT. I effectively ran the company for the entire integration time and joined all the dots. I understood how it all hangs together. (Senior manager, FTSE 100 company)

Innovation and vision

Change can be achieved either by meeting a minimum of requirements or by being bold and visionary. The interviewees talked about how they created ambitious visions for the area they were changing and how they had to rally people behind this vision. Being progressive, innovative and bold are characteristics that are valued by companies but can also make the change effort more difficult, as those affected by it are more likely to resist the changes:

> I professionalized the area and built my own team, which had a different profile from the traditional company profile. I built a team with people from diverse backgrounds, such as investment banking and consultancy. My people have now moved on to senior roles in [the organization]. Also, nobody else at the time was thinking about the internet and using technology. My contribution was the introduction of different working methodologies, looking abroad for different technology and benchmarking. I got a lot of visibility at the age of 27. Those were hard-working years and I was investing in my career. (Senior manager, FTSE 100 company)

SUPPORT

Both managers and sponsors can provide support by believing in the woman who is running the organizational change assignment. While they give high-level directions about what needs to be done, they leave her to work out for herself a strategy and solutions, and allow her to stretch herself. Sponsors and managers also have an important role to play in being advocates for the organizational change assignment the woman is running, as the resistance that change agents face is substantial and may at times feel insurmountable. Sponsors and managers also provide access to senior stakeholder groups, which help a woman to obtain the buy-in she needs for her proposed plans. Furthermore, managers and sponsors also provide indirect support by being role models showing how to navigate the political challenges a woman may encounter during times of change and upheaval. Observing others interacting while lines of power are redrawn is an important lesson. A small number of interviewees also stressed the importance of being able to talk through events at work with their partners.

TIMING

It is never too early to try one's hand at improving existing work processes; however, large-scale organizational change projects that have an impact on significant parts of an organization demand a solid foundation in stakeholder management and implementation tenacity. They are therefore best tackled once these foundations are in place, from middle management level onwards. Many of the middle managers talked about the increasingly large change projects they had been entrusted with more recently. These projects are still relatively clearly defined and mainly managed by the interviewees themselves without a team reporting to them. The projects put a woman in contact with all the important challenges of change management she will come across in large-scale, less well-defined assignments later in her career. Those interviewees who had managed large-scale organizational change projects relied on their excellent stakeholder management skills and political nous in order to overcome resistance and implementation hurdles.

SUMMARY

A significant number of the interviewees described themselves as change agents, a quality that is valued by their organizations. Along with being a turnaround pro and an intrapreneur, being a change agent is one of the areas of leadership expertise that women tend to fall into. A number of the interviewees have made their names by being effective implementers of organizational change. The In Focus section highlighted the importance of these making-your-name assignments that help a woman to stand out and facilitate her move to senior management roles.

The interviewees talked at length about the challenges associated with dealing with the various emotions associated with change. Their second big challenge was dealing with the uncertainty that organizational change often brings, and with not having enough information on which to base decisions. The interviewees talked about learning to make decisions on the best available information, and about the importance of taking action rather than waiting for more information to become available. The women-specific challenges focused on dealing with male chauvinism and paternalistic thinking. Not surprisingly, helping others to deal with change, and learning about the importance of ongoing communication were the important lessons the interviewees took away with them. The career benefits of organizational change assignments are closely liked to delivering performance-changing outcomes and being a proven change agent with a holistic understanding of an organization and a drive to innovate. Once solid project management skills are in place, managers should try their hand at their first, smaller-scale change management project. Senior managers who take on organization-wide change efforts need to rely on solid stakeholder management skills, political nous and implementation tenacity to make a project one of their making-your-name assignments.

TAKING ACTION

- **Your signature strength.** Do you enjoy improving business processes and instigating change? Do you often find fault with the status quo and are keen to change it? Consider whether change management could become your signature strength, which will allow you to make your name and stand out from the crowd.
- **Gaining maximum visibility.** What types of organizational change have you already mastered? Is this the type of change the company values? Before choosing your next organizational change assignment, assess whether it will give you maximum visibility.
- **Being a change agent.** If you are new to change management, which challenges are you most likely to find difficult? The 'people side', such as dealing with people's reactions to proposed plans, and appealing to people's emotions when you are communicating the need and vision for the proposed changes? Or the 'rational side', such as finding the right type of information, and making decisions based on limited information? Strengthen the areas with which you feel less comfortable.

11

DEALING WITH PROBLEMS AND CRISES: THE TURNAROUND PRO

Women can be too earnest, which makes people uneasy. Don't be too earnest but be brave about the moments where you feel passionate and go for it.

(Amanda MacKenzie, Group Marketing Director, Aviva)

You need to work out what you are really good at and have utter faith in it.

(Carolyn Fairbairn,
Group Development and Strategy Director, ITV)

Being a proven turnaround expert is one of the ways in which women can make their name and stand out from the crowd. Turnaround experts deal with urgent crisis situations that require immediate and drastic action. In these crisis situations, market share is plummeting fast, large sums of money are being lost every day, or customers are leaving the company in droves. While all assignments have to be executed with pace, turnaround projects are a step up from the more orderly and proactive organizational change assignments discussed in Chapter 10. Turnaround assignments demand an immediate stabilization of a situation and the demonstration of rapid results. They are a particular form of organizational change, and Slatter and colleagues refer to them as 'radical short-term change which delivers fast financial gain' (p. xii).[1]

There is evidence that, when women take on senior leadership positions, they take them on with a turnaround remit. A positive explanation for this observation is that women's leadership style equips them well to deal with such precarious situations. A McKinsey survey found that the leadership behaviors that were displayed more frequently by women, such as setting clear expectations, acting as role models and using inspiration, were also more effective during and after crises.[2] One of the interviewees also pointed out that women's practical approach often makes them good candidates for dealing with turnaround situations because they 'just get on with it'. The following comment echoes this view:

> I see in my life women who are good at this. Women are more practical in crisis situations. They are sensible and they are good fixers. In a male-dominated environment, women look at problems in a different way and are operationally quite sensible. This experience gives women confidence and credibility. (Anna Capitanio, Vice-President, Organizational Effectiveness and M&A HR, BT Global Services)

A less positive explanation is the 'glass cliff', a term coined by Ryan and Haslam and based on a series of studies which show that organizations that have been facing difficulties for some time are more likely to appoint women to leadership positions.[3] A US study also found that those Fortune 500 companies that had in recent years experienced a reputational, legal or financial scandal were more likely to have female CEOs than those that had not experienced such scandals.[4] As Ryan and Haslam point out, women who are appointed to senior positions in organizations with financial or other forms of problems may attract unwarranted criticism, as failing results are attributed to the woman and her leadership style rather than the overall precarious situation.

A number of the senior women I interviewed described themselves as turnaround experts. The types of assignments they talked about included rescuing failing implementation projects, sorting out under-performing operations centers, and dealing with over-expanded businesses. The following comments provide an example of the challenges and learning that two senior interviewees experienced. These accounts are representative of many of the other interviewees' experiences:

> I moved into a wider leadership role and had to make tough decisions as this was a critical time for the business. The dot.com bubble had burst and the business had over-expanded. It was difficult to run a company and at the time I didn't know what I didn't know. I moved from a functional role to a wider business role but I had the benefit of business curiosity and always knew about the wider business context; I used all my energy to find out about things. I used

humility and spent long hours trying to understand. But then comes a time when you have to take action. I had to do a number of significant restructures such as closing, opening and selling businesses and [making] major redundancies, winning new business and setting up loans. (Senior manager, FTSE 100 company)

It was a turnaround role with P&L accountability. I had to find the right customers for [the organization's] products. I had to create an environment where everyone got on in the team and where the team pulled together. There could be no more back-biting. I had to line people up behind my new strategy. I had to find the right solutions for customers and make progress while lots of changes were afoot. I had to change the management team, move office and create exports to various countries. I turned revenues from $10m to $100m. (Senior manager, FTSE 100 company)

These roles are urgent and the stakes are high. They are obtained almost exclusively through personal contacts and informal conversations within the organization. Crisis situations are not a time for hiring new people. Senior managers are looking for a safe pair of hands and an established track record; most often they turn to people they have worked with in the past. Many of the interviewees mentioned that being known for always delivering and being 100 percent dedicated to achieving results helped when they were being considered for a turnaround assignment:

He gave me the role because he knew that I would deliver, that I like taking responsibility and show personal commitment. I take action after I have come to a conclusion. I have a sense of fearlessness and I try not to get intimidated by things. (Margaret Johnson, Group CEO, Leagas Delaney)

'I didn't know what I didn't know', 'I didn't know just how much of a mess it all was' – the interviewees admitted to not having a complete grasp of just how desperate the situation was when they took on the assignment. And all the women who admitted this were glad that they hadn't known the full extent of the challenge as they would not have taken on the role had they known. The roles were described as impossible situations in a few cases, but nevertheless the women managed to turn them around to great acclaim. Slatter and colleagues set out a series of key activities associated with successful turnaround situations: (a) active key stakeholder engagement; (b) strong leadership and ownership of the crisis situation; (c) bringing on board a new leadership team; (d) creating a sense of urgency and highlighting the need for immediate results; (e) communicating an overall vision; (f) taking action on the most urgent areas that need to be fixed; and (g) putting in place new processes and structures. We shall come across most of these elements in the next few sections. The interviewees referred to some of these activities when they talked about the challenges associated with turnaround situations, and to others when they talked about the lessons learned or the career benefits gained from this critical job assignment.

JOB-SPECIFIC CHALLENGES

There are three main types of challenges the interviewees mentioned when they talked about their turnaround experience; first, taking action fast and fixing things; second, reengaging people; and finally, working in a broken environment. The most prominent of these themes was taking action fast and fixing things. This is not surprising, given the crisis element of turnaround assignments and the need to stabilize a situation quickly.

Acting quickly and fixing problems

Before the interviewees began to take specific action they had to work out dependencies between work streams and establish the biggest risks and priorities. However, this was quickly followed by making tough decisions and taking action. The interviewees emphasized the need to take action promptly and the danger of getting bogged down in overanalyzing a situation. They also talked at length about the different things they had to fix and the actions they had to take to stabilize the situation. These actions were at times very specific, such as finding new customers, creating export routes to new countries, moving or closing offices, making redundancies, or undergoing refinancing of some sort. Other actions were linked to people decisions; for example, restructuring teams or creating an environment where people worked together better than they had in the past. The need for rapid action creates a pressurized work environment, and the interviewees talked about how difficult their turnaround experiences had been: 'This was my toughest time. The hours were horrendous' (Senior manager, FTSE 100 company).

Re-establishing commitment

By the time a woman takes on a turnaround assignment, many different stakeholders may have become disillusioned in response to the developing crisis. Engaging people, and subsequently galvanizing them behind necessary action, is vital. Formulating a vision and gaining others' buy-in and trust are also important.[5]

> I had to work out dependencies between work streams and think ahead. The project was not thinking far enough ahead and had no vision about how to get to the end. This meant that the team and the stakeholders had lost commitment and had stopped believing that it could be achieved. Also, the key stakeholders had changed during the project. I had to understand my priorities and biggest risks, and I had to get a higher-level vision for the jigsaw pieces so people could believe that it could be done. I also had to become influential and develop a track record. Once you have delivered you can be trusted to do the same again. You need to be consistent in what you do and wear your brand. I had to do lots of rebuilding of relationships during the organizational change period but you cannot hurry trust along. You can maybe hurry it a bit through quick wins and a lot of consistency. (Wendy Antaw, Head of Information Systems, Land Securities Group)

Working in a broken environment

Working in a broken environment can make it difficult to achieve the fast results that are needed to deal with a crisis. While an obvious crisis, or 'burning platform' as they are sometimes called, make the need for change very clear and help to galvanize employees' actions, the existence of an acute crises also creates anxiety, narrows people's attention span, and creates tunnel vision. Anxiety makes us revert to our comfort zones and while it may motivate us to work harder, it may also stop people from embracing the new ways of working that are often necessary to turn around a situation with sustainable, long-term benefits.[6] The interviewees talked about experiences, such as a lack of cooperation between

164

teams, and writing emails rather than having conversations as a way of covering one's back. They also talked about bosses who were on edge, untrusting or too involved in the work that needed to be done. Breaking strikes and dealing with internal back-biting were also mentioned.

> This was my first non-financial role. It was not my cup of tea. It was in a mess. Everybody thought I had come in to close it down. Morale was bad, there were lots of broken systems and processes. I had never stood up in front of so many people [over 400] before and I had to change quickly. I put it on my list to walk the floor. I had to get people to change things and give them self-belief. (Senior manager, FTSE 100 company)

> At the starting point of a new venture people are positive and there are projections of hope. However, if something is in distress, there is mostly a negative point of view and people become very defensive. (CEO, UK company)

Working in a broken environment also means that nothing is well-defined, and when the turnaround phase starts, the true scale of the problems is often not clear. One interviewee talked about how the scope of her role grew significantly after she had taken on the assignment. She was initially asked to turn around one particular work stream that was in difficulty. At that time she was responsible for two people but within two months the project scope grew and she was asked to take on the entire project and with it a team of 40.

WOMEN-SPECIFIC CHALLENGES

She shouldn't have this role

When successful women progress to senior management roles, which often happens earlier than for men, as we saw in Chapter 2, they are often faced with older men in their team who feel that they should not be in the role. The comment below talks about how a male CEO initially boycotted a woman's work as he felt that, as a young woman, she should not have been given a senior turnaround role:

> The CEO of the company was an established gentleman, very senior. I was sent as a young female to talk to staff. The first weeks

were awful as he took exception to me being female. He didn't help me. Then we had a pivotal meeting where I listened to him and I shared my expertise. I asked him: 'Can you help me do this? You have many years of experience.' Afterwards he became a mentor for me. (Senior manager, FTSE 100 company)

Another interviewee talked about having to establish herself as a leader after being asked to take a management role. One of the senior men in the team felt that he should have had the job. The second part of her comment is representative of the feelings of other interviewees, who maintained that they have not experienced any women-specific challenges but then go on to mention a number of additional difficulties.

I had a senior guy working for me who thought that he should have had the role not me. But generally I have never experienced anything that has stopped me. Maybe only first impressions when people say 'Oh, she is a woman.' (Senior manager, FTSE 100 company)

IN FOCUS: SENSITIVITY

Are women more emotional and sensitive than their male counterparts at work or is this only a stereotype? A significant number of the interviewees agreed that women are in fact more sensitive and more emotional. As they progress in their careers and become more senior, they seem to take away three important lessons. First, accept that you are likely to react more emotionally and be prepared to ensure that your emotions don't take you by surprise. Second, develop a thick skin! And finally, when you are dealing with men, emotions need to be kept in check as men find it difficult to deal with them. Let us look at these points in turn. I shall use a lot of quotes from the interviews as they are very powerful demonstrations of these three points. The following comment is a good illustration of what the interviewees mentioned in relation to women's sensitivity and high level of emotionality:

You cannot change women's psyche. Our sensitivity is part of us. You don't need to leave it behind but you need full body armour on occasions. It is not personal and women mustn't be too sensitive.

(Sophie Turner Laing, Managing Director, Entertainment and News, British Sky Broadcasting)

Leading on from here is the second lesson to be learned: developing a thick skin. The majority of the interviewees mentioned this in one form or another. They talked about developing a thick skin in the context of ignoring inappropriate remarks or behavior, dealing with rejection or criticism, and being brave enough to speak up and ask for more even if the answer is likely to be 'no'.

If something sexist happens, take the emotion away. You need to get on with it and be pragmatic, and you need to accept that things are not perfect and develop a thick skin. If you want to achieve you need to be able to navigate around the politics and deal with complex political situations. (Mary Lawrance, Founder, Cariance Executive Search)

Not all ideas are accepted and you need a thick skin. You need confidence to put your opinion out there. Men expect things to come their way. Women are more aware of their vulnerabilities and more sensitive to situations. You need high IQ and EQ, and you need to understand situations. (Lois Wark, Group Corporate Communications Manager, Randgold Resources)

During these earlier roles I learnt to develop a thick skin and not to take things personally. If you don't ask you don't get. You need to be resilient. (Senior manager, FTSE 100 company)

The interviewees referred to men's discomfort with emotions and because of this learned to interact with them in a more rational manner:

Men are unemotional and struggle with emotions; it makes them uncomfortable. My emotions are written on my face so I use a calming technique to get the courage to ask calmly for a pay rise, for example. (Senior manager, FTSE 100 company)

When it comes to banter and jokes about women, the interviewees talked about the importance of integrity and knowing oneself. How far will I go with it? At the same time, having a light-touch way of challenging rather than making a big deal out of it seems to work best for most women. It is a balancing act and something that the interviewees seemed to have acquired over time and through some trial and error:

> Sometimes people make feminist jokes but it is only for fun. I play it down rather than make a big deal out of it. I think I'm quite lucky because I have a genuine interest in cars and sport, and this allows me to engage in many of the out of work conversations. (Senior manager, FTSE 100 company)

> If people want to have a joke about me being woman in a certain situation, I will do it. You need to have a light-touch challenge. But you need to have a sense of self: 'This is me. I can only go so far beyond that.' You need integrity. (Senior manager, FTSE 100 company)

LESSONS LEARNED

Crisis management

Crisis management is the most prominent lesson from turnaround situations. When turnaround managers start their work this is what they usually meet straight away – a crisis that has to be stabilized as quickly as possible. In addition to conserving cash in the immediate future, rebuilding stakeholder confidence is another vital objective of this phase:[7]

> It allowed me to become confident in my own abilities. I enjoyed being abroad. It provided me with the foundation of abilities such as risk assessment, time prioritization and calling for help. (Jo Pisani, Partner, PricewaterhouseCoopers)

> [The assignment] taught me crisis management. Any really competent person needs to be able to deal with crises. During this role I also learned that it is very important to have good people. The more senior you are, the more you need to create an environment for others to run the business rather than doing it yourself – lobbying, recognizing the value of professional skills and experience. You need to have well-qualified people working for you. You also need to have a vision for the company; it is no longer just management. (CEO, UK company)

I learned most from the biggest disasters. I learned how to mobilize people and seek alliances. How to win the support of those originally opposed to me. I learned about the importance of being honest – say what you don't know. I learned to get the home team under control and get everyone singing off the same hymn sheet. I learned to negotiate contracts and who to trust and who not to trust. How to take an expert briefing on anything in half an hour. How to choose your advisors wisely, and how to have consistent and clear leadership so your team trusts you. You need to get the team to pull together and discuss contentious issues behind closed doors. (Jenny Newton, Senior manager, Information Technology industry)

As can be seen from the comments above, crisis management has two distinct elements to it: first, leadership; and second, project planning and implementation. The leadership style that is often regarded as the most effective in times of crisis is very different from the style advocated for more stable times. While there is now general agreement that autocratic leadership styles do not work, the accepted exception is the turnaround assignment. When operations are failing and money is being lost, decisive action and clear, directive leadership are of the essence. Crisis management also contains an element of rapid project planning:

In a project space you can never have enough contingencies for people. There are three elements you can vary: time, quality and cost. You can only ever change one of these parameters at any one time. (Senior manager, FTSE 100 company)

It is imperative that you sort out existing problems ... you will not give yourself headroom to move on if you do not sort out the fundamentals in your area' (Gillian Berkmen, Group Brand and Commercial Director, Mothercare)

Finally, more than one area is likely to need attention at the same time; and with all areas seeming urgent, prioritizing is essential.

Leading in times of crisis

The leadership element of crisis management has already been discussed briefly above, but as leadership in times of a crisis is often very different from leading in stable times, it deserves a closer look. Isern and colleagues point to the importance of strong leadership in turnaround situations.[8] They refer to the findings of a McKinsey global survey which shows that defensive transformations succeed only about a third of the time. Important elements of strong leadership are setting clearly defined stretch targets, creating local ownership for the necessary transformations, and strong personal involvement and visibility of the senior leader in charge of the organizational change assignment.

The most important of these characteristics of leadership is setting a stretch target. This is linked directly to the interviewees' accounts of having to develop a clear and inspirational vision of the turnaround project in order to reestablish stakeholder commitment. Isern and his colleagues also point out that effective turnaround experts not only have to address stretch targets, local ownership and personal involvement, but also implement these effectively. This emphasis on implementation is further reinforced by Slatter and Lovett, who see effective turnaround experts as having both good leadership and good management skills.[9] Their list of desirable qualities for a turnaround expert is long and they compare it to being a good general manager but one who has to make tougher decisions under more time pressure. We heard about the importance of learning to make decisions in Chapter 6, which explored operational experience and running a business. Turnaround assignments allow a woman to further hone her decision-making skills in a tough and time-pressured situation, as the following comment shows: 'I learned that the most important thing in a leadership role is to be respected, even if you have to make tough decisions and people no longer like you. It's OK as long as you keep their respect' (Margaret Johnson, Group CEO, Leagas Delaney).

Putting in place new processes

After the crisis has been averted and the situation has been stabilized it may be tempting to move on to the next turnaround assignment. The interviewees who had run a number of large-scale turnaround projects stressed the importance of putting in place new processes before moving on. Without new processes in place, the changes that were implemented to rescue a business or a failing project are unlikely to become embedded, and as a result the turnaround efforts themselves may sooner or later be lost. Interestingly, the people who run the turnaround phase and those who put in place new processes are not always the same, as different skills are needed.[10] The interviewees pointed out that they had to make sure the organization was in a position to implement the new processes, and that the right person for this task had to be found. The following two comments highlight these points:

> I also learned to put processes in place. I had to find the right people to do that for me. I recognized that if you are a process person you are unlikely to be a turnaround person. However, if you don't put in place processes as a turnaround person it was all in vain. You have to find the right person to do it for you. (Jenny Newton, Senior Manager, Information Technology industry)

> I learned to manage organizational change and to make sure that the business has the skills to transition to new processes. I now point to possible risks of a project failing much earlier than I have done in the past. (Senior manager, FTSE 100 company)

CAREER BENEFITS

Delivering results

The outcomes of turnaround assignments are usually very visible, because large-scale change has taken place. The interviewees talked at length about how turning around a failing project or business unit allowed them to demonstrate tangible outcomes and benefits for the organization. They increased revenues tenfold, renegotiated unprofitable customer contracts, won new business, moved businesses out of debt, attracted new talent and obtained high feedback scores on the staff survey for their functions. These results are very quantifiable and the achievements are easy for everyone to see:

> Others recognize that I can take responsibility and that I am accountable. The business is now in very good shape commercially. Now we have great top talent in the organization and we are expanding again. (Margaret Johnson, CEO, Leagas Delaney)

In addition to these very specific results, the women demonstrated highly valued commitment and accountability.

Commitment and accountability

Commitment and accountability are two related qualities which the interviewees demonstrated during turnaround projects and which helped them to further build their track record and to prove themselves to be a safe pair of hands in difficult situations. Accountability applies both to showing that a woman is holding her team to account and managing the team's performance effectively, as well as confirming her own accountability for the ultimate outcome of the assignment. With this comes 100 percent commitment to making the assignment a success:

> I created a legacy and demonstrated that I am highly driven. I never let go. They saw the change in me and my broadening of perspective. (Senior manager, FTSE 100 company)

> My [boss] handed me a crying baby. What did he see in me when he gave me the role? … I have an interest in business and I maintain perspective. I have a plan B, which means I cannot be held to ransom. (Senior manager, FTSE 100 company)

> I showed the organization that I can lead, that I am committed and that I see things through. It allowed me to build genuine relationships which have substance to them and I was able to debate and talk and wasn't too cautious about what I said and thought. I also gave my boss the confidence that I would make it as much of a success as he needed it to be. I got a lot of internal respect as people believed that I could do it. (Wendy Antaw, Head of Information Systems, Land Securities Group)

SUPPORT

Managers have an important role to play in supporting a woman during a turnaround assignment. While some of the interviewees mentioned that they relished the opportunity to just get on with it and sort things out, a woman's manager can add value by acting as a sponsor and key advocate for the need of the turnaround assignment. They fulfill the important role of convincing key stakeholders that turnaround is the best solution for the problems the company is facing. He or she can help to create a sense of urgency and to secure resources for the turnaround pro.

We have already heard in Chapter 8 about the importance of having a good team. However, given the pressurized situations in which women find themselves during turnaround times, a good team is just as important, if not more so, here.

TIMING

Turnaround situations tend to take place later in a woman's career. An understanding of how business works and how change is implemented successfully are important foundations to give a woman a realistic chance of succeeding at turning around a failing business. The women I talked to also outlined the importance of contacts. These contacts provide expertise in an area where the woman may still have to find her feet. They also act as a sounding board, which is an important support feature in crisis situations as a woman's boss may be very hands-off:

> You need to have successful examples and foundations in place to be able to handle a turnaround situation. To turn something around that is business-critical you need experience and contacts. (Wendy Antaw, Head of Information Systems, Land Securities Group)

Early exposure to turnaround situations is, of course, beneficial. Working with people who are regarded as effective turnaround professionals allows a woman to understand which behaviors are important and which are not. Looking for smaller, well-defined change projects that will equip a woman with some of the change management skills which play a big part in turnaround programs will put her in a good position for tackling her first turnaround project.

SUMMARY

Turnaround projects are arguably one of the most challenging types of assignments. They are led by people who have proved themselves to be a safe pair of hands and who are seen as committed and willing to take full accountability for the assignment. These projects are typically encountered at middle to senior management level, as a woman needs to have a solid basis of change management and leadership skills, as well as relationships, to fall back on. Nevertheless, early exposure to smaller, more self-contained turnaround projects with strong managerial support are a good starting point for more junior women. Running a turnaround project requires grit and determination, and this is no time to feel sensitive. The In Focus section talked about the difference in men's and women's level of emotionality, and the need to equip oneself with strong armour and a thick skin. The women-specific challenges emerged when senior men took exception to a younger woman being in a senior management role. Turnaround projects take place in a broken environment where senior stakeholders have lost commitment, bosses are on edge and people cover their own backs. Crisis management is the main lesson taken away from this experience, with both its leadership and project management elements. A woman's manager is most helpful when he or she is confident enough in the turnaround pro's ability to let her deal with the situation on her own as much as she feels comfortable to do, while at the same time providing support with important senior-level lobbying on her behalf.

TAKING ACTION

- **Bringing together management and leadership skills.** Turnaround assignments are a fabulous opportunity for a woman to demonstrate a strong combination of effective management and inspirational leadership. Are both your implementation skills as well as your inspirational people leadership skills strong enough to take on a pressurized change management situation? If not, consider the areas in which you have to gain more experience.
- **A reliable deliverer of results.** Turnaround assignments are most likely to be given to people in the organization that have shown themselves to be a safe pair of hands at delivering results in difficult situations. How well connected are you with people who are making appointment decisions in this area? What are the characteristics of the people who are currently entrusted with turnaround situations? How does your skill set compare to these turnaround pros?

12

JOINING THE EXECUTIVE COMMITTEE: MAKING IT TO THE TOP

People who have made it to the top haven't had a smooth ride. They have messed something up. Women can take it very personally. Men are better at externalizing. Be more male and blame the environment – something was not right. It is important to bounce back and keep going.
(Helen Buck, Convenience Director, J. Sainsbury)

There is a point in women's lives when they see others going to the top and they ask themselves why not me? I can do this, too.
(Sheelagh Whittaker, Non-Executive Director, Standard Life)

Joining the executive committee[1] of a FTSE 100 company is an impressive achievement for anyone, and particularly so for women. The women who make it join a small number of other women already at this level. As we saw in the Introduction, the percentage of women in senior decision-making roles is small. Only 20 percent of senior management positions across the world are held by women, and the G7 countries lag behind this global average with only 16 percent of senior management positions being held by women.[2] Cranfield University's *Female FTSE Board Report* shows that only 22 percent of senior management positions in the UK are held by women, and if we are looking at FTSE 100 directorships the numbers are even smaller – only 5.5 percent of executive directorships (a total of 18 positions) are held by women, and only 12 percent if female non-executive directors are included in these numbers. Let us take a look at two more examples. Across Germany's 200 largest companies, only 3.2 percent of executive directorships are held by women.[3] In the USA, 14.4 percent of Fortune 500 executive officer positions are held by women, as are 15.7 percent of Fortune 500 corporate board seats.[4] The numbers are still disappointing, and only in countries where legislation to increase the percentage of women in senior positions has been introduced, such as Norway, are there substantially more women at the top. Various reports and research studies point to the benefits of women being part of executive committees in organizations. The results of a McKinsey study, for example, show a relationship between women's representation in senior management teams and the organization's performance.[5] In a follow-on study they showed that women use five of the nine leadership behaviors linked to organizational performance more frequently than did their male colleagues.[6] For real benefits to be felt, though, there seems to be a critical mass of three or more women in a senior management team before their status moves from being a woman to being a fully accepted and integrated team member whose gender does not matter.

Why is this last chapter about moving to an executive committee role rather than becoming an executive director or even a CEO? As with all the chapters in the book, it has been led by what the interviewees said were critical job assignments for them, and moving to an executive committee role was the most senior role the interviewees talked about. While the sample also includes a number of current and former CEOs and a number of executive and non-executive directors, and while a small number of these interviewees talked about the challenges of moving to non-executive director positions, the data set for joining a FTSE 100 executive committee is larger and richer. This is not surprising, as the majority of women at the top of organizations still progress there via a functional route, as we saw in Chapter 6. For senior managers with a functional background, being part of the executive committee is in many cases as far as their lack of general management experience will allow them to go as executives. From that point, many women progress by acquiring non-executive directorships.

JOB-SPECIFIC CHALLENGES

A big step up

A few of the interviewees talked about taking big steps up when they discussed moving to an executive committee position:

> This was a big leap for me. I had a lot of new areas of responsibility and there were different personalities I had to deal with. I had

been safe in my last organization and now I had to reestablish my network and work out who to trust and who not to trust. (Senior manager, FTSE 100 organization)

I was suddenly catapulted into running a big team and to facing upwards. I hadn't been a great delegator and had to become better at that straight away. I was suddenly a known name, and for someone relatively quiet it felt that I was exposed and I felt observed by the organization. I was thinking 'I am visible now!' (Carolyn Fairbairn, Group Development and Strategy Director, ITV)

One senior manager talked about moving to her second executive committee role in a new organization:

I took a big step up … It was a new culture and board team but I never worried about not being able to do it. I've got to learn and listen, work hard but I can do it. I worked around the clock in the first year. (Kate Bostock, Executive Director, General Merchandise, Marks & Spencer)

With this big step up came some initial self-doubt for some of the interviewees as to whether the new role could be mastered. The challenge the interviewees mentioned most frequently was having to focus on other areas of the business outside their own function to get a better understanding of the total business. Other business challenges mentioned were quite specific, such as having to restructure a function or division, having to introduce pioneering processes, or dealing with a fast pace of acquisitions.

A small, in-depth study conducted by Odgers Berndtson with 32 of Germany's 49 top executive women found that more than half of these women reported this last step to join the executive to be the most difficult because of the generally held perceptions about women becoming senior leaders.[7] The numbers in the study underpinning this book are small, but interestingly, without being asked explicitly about it, a few of the interviewees also reported that they had been doing more career planning recently than ever before. Moving to an executive committee, and then, in particular, the next step to a woman's first executive or non-executive directorship, are steps that take time, resilience and persistence as well as some well-thought-through actions and networking.

Integrating with the executive team

As newly appointed members of the executive team, the interviewees were the outsiders who had to take proactive steps to integrate into the team as quickly as possible. This is very much about building new relationships, understanding how the existing team works and finding a style of contributing that works in this new setting. One senior executive mentioned that she had been advised to make sure that, after joining a new executive committee she should spend time 'getting in with the new executive team and gelling with them'. While her direct team would also be new to her, she was advised that this team could wait, and that it was more important to build the senior relationships first in order to deal with the business challenges in her role. She outlined how she spent the first three months focusing on building relationships with important senior colleagues such as the HR director and the finance director. These strong relationships later helped her to turn around the part of the organization for which she was responsible. Another senior executive talked about how she had to take the initiative when building relationships at the senior level:

> I haven't experienced any women-specific issues. But don't get me wrong, I am the one who has worked on building relationships. They [the men] have not come to knock on my door. (Gillian Berkmen, Group Brand and Commercial Director, Mothercare)

> I have always been the only woman in management teams, but being the lawyer helps as people expect you to be bright and well-educated. You are also an advisor to senior people. You may have to give difficult advice but that gains you respect. Generally, to gain respect you need to take time to understand all the stakeholders and the key here is preparation, preparation and preparation. You cannot wing it when you are talking to senior people. (Senior manager, FTSE 100 company)

The interviewees talked at length about building relationships and how the difference between women's and men's style of interaction can create barriers which have to be overcome; and they are mainly overcome by the women, who had to take the first step to build the relationships.

IN FOCUS: NETWORKING WITH MEN

In Chapter 3 we heard about the importance of networking as part of a woman's career progression strategies, the benefits that networking brings and the challenges women face when it comes to accessing the right types of networks. This In Focus section provides a personalized account of what it feels like for women to network with men. A number of the women's comments in this section are very revealing and explain to some extent why women find it more difficult to network with men. The first comment provides a great overview of how one female senior manager initially struggled with networking events but slowly learned to feel more comfortable by acquiring certain 'networking with men' techniques. Her comment is fairly representative of what the other interviewees had to say:

> I found the networking at male-dominated events very difficult to start with. At dinners and drinks it was 99 percent men. It was particularly difficult as I was a young woman. Eventually it became easier and I became more confident but I didn't enjoy big group settings. I am still not that great at them now. But I am no longer fazed by going to these events. The problem is the sense of not having anything in common. I get around this by striking up a conversation on topics that men have something to say about, such as sport – something they are interested in. It may not be something you want to talk about but you need to do it in order to move on the conversation. With men you need to think harder and be prepared. I tend to comment on the most recent sporting event and that mostly appeals to men, or I talk about the most recent business deal. Men don't like personal questions. Men tend to comment on an issue or an event. They rarely talk about themselves to start with. They are happiest when they are giving an observation about something. Often they are scared to talk to women. They think 'Oh dear, there is a woman coming, what shall I say?' You cannot wait for them to strike up a conversation as they won't. You need to ask a number of questions to warm them up. With women the conversation starts quickly. (Senior manager, FTSE 100 company)

Having something in common to share is a widely recognized hurdle and one that women overcome by talking about 'male' subjects such as sport or cars:

> Networking starts to feed on itself; you need to get to a critical mass to get introductions via your network. Networking with men is harder as we are built differently. People herd together around common interests. Guys don't talk about anything personal whereas women do. Guys have a bunch of topics that allow them to galvanize. Football allows them to interact but without having to reveal anything personal. I have always talked about work as a shared topic. (Jessica Burley, CEO of MCHI)

One interviewee described how she feels when the conversation moves from business as a shared topic to a purely social conversation:

> With someone you talk to every day, once you are in a social setting, it's like they are talking a different language. Men have their little phrases and catchwords. Suddenly you feel like all your power is gone and you feel like an outsider. (Senior manager, FTSE 100 company)

But the interviewees, particularly the most senior ones in the sample, recognize the importance of networking and the importance of 'going for it', as the comment below shows:

> Networking is incredibly important. I see it as building relationships in a spirit of 'paying it forward'. Think about it as 'netgiving'. Men sit in a huddle and you feel like you are interrupting. Use the energy of being really good at one-to-one relationships and be thick-skinned. Women can be too earnest, which makes people uneasy. Don't be too earnest, but be brave about the moments where you feel passionate and go for it. Be yourself. Change happens one conversation at a time. Build relationships. Just do it, face it, knock down stereotypes. Men always have sport to talk about – you need to build one-to-one relationships so it is easier when you are in a group with them, and that doesn't mean you need to talk sport! (Amanda MacKenzie, Group Marketing Director, Aviva)

Many of the interviewees talked about the importance of building one-to-one relationships in order to feel more comfortable and to have more of a voice when in a group of men. Despite the challenges women encounter with the 'old boys' network', it can have advantages for women, too: 'The old boys' network is the best help for women to get support and sponsorship. Everyone [senior male leaders] should pick one or two women to support and sponsor' (Helen Mahy, Company Secretary and General Counsel, National Grid).

The interviewees agreed that male senior leaders need to take a more proactive role in including women in senior teams as the following comments show:

'It is not about fixing the women. It is enabling the men to feel more comfortable with women. It is not the women who need to get the training' (Senior manager, FTSE 100 company).

Another senior interviewee echoed these words by outlining how it is a senior leader's role to bring everyone in his or her team into the conversation:

> There is an unintentional bias. Women are often seen as not being ambitious. There is a lack of inclusion at senior management level as people recruit in their own likeness. At National Grid everybody is going through inclusiveness training. If you are the leader of a group you ought to bring everybody in. In big meetings, young and junior women are nervous about speaking up and are seen as stupid. Inclusiveness training is like safety training; it has to be delivered from board level downward and needs to be continually reinforced to send a message – 'This is the organization we are.' (Helen Mahy, Company Secretary and General Counsel, National Grid)

Finding your voice (again)

This point is closely related to the previous one of integrating with the existing executive committee, but it is dealt with separately as it is a matter of inner confidence rather than of externally adapting one's working styles. A number of the interviewees talked about the time they first attended board meetings and how they felt nervous, how they remained quiet initially during the meetings in order to observe what was going on, and how they felt somewhat intimidated. This initial level of nervousness is not surprising, given that these women had just moved to the uppermost echelons of large FTSE 100 companies. All the interviewees were very open about their initial apprehension. Let us look at what some of the interviewees said when they joined an executive committee for the first time:

> This role gave me my first exposure to board meetings. I was initially nervous but I grew confident. (Senior manager, FTSE 100 company)

> I was the new person. Nobody knew me ... At lunches and breakout sessions I built relationships with the new team. It was a bit intimidating but I enjoyed it. (Senior manager, FTSE 100 company)

> I was the only woman there. For the first month I was conscious of it. You have to be more selective with what you say because you need to be perceived in a certain way. You have to show sensitivity and have to weigh things up. You cannot just go in to criticize – you need to offer an alternative. (Senior manager, FTSE 100 company)

> On the executive committee everybody has a job to do and nobody is isolated. Everybody has opinions. Anything that adds extra value is well received. But not all ideas are accepted and ... you need confidence to put your opinion out there. People get to know you and appreciate your input. (Lois Wark, Group Corporate Communications Manager, Randgold Resources)

As we shall see in the Lessons Learned section below, these initial doubts did not remain for long and the interviewees soon found their voices and confidence again.

WOMEN-SPECIFIC CHALLENGES

A vote of confidence

We have already encountered establishing credibility as a job-specific challenge in other critical job assignments: in Chapter 4 as part of an early stretch assignment; in Chapter 6 when moving to a new environment; and in Chapter 10 as part of creating a new business venture. These are all situations where a woman is either an unknown quantity (as in an early stretch assignment or when working in a new environment) or the outcomes of her proposed plans are so uncertain that buy-in is only likely if the woman herself is seen as highly credible (for example, when putting forward ideas for a new business venture). We also heard about it as a women-specific challenge in Chapter 4. Despite having reached the top of an organization, credibility-building still remains an issue for women, particularly when they have just joined from a different company to take up a new executive committee role. Let us see whether the interviewee's experience has changed at all compared to Chapter 4:

> The CEO said that he had got support from the executive team for me to join the team. He had the team vote on me joining. However, I have since seen men join the team who have not required a vote from the others. (Senior manager, FTSE 100 company)

This next comment is from a female executive who joined a start-up as its new CEO. She also talked about the importance of establishing credibility with the new team:

> As a woman I had to say things twice. I had to make myself visible and participate in discussions. They didn't expect much of me, as I was new. I always prepared very well so that I could contribute. (Anne-Mette Øvrum, Property Manager, Kongsvinger kommune)

This next comment was not in connection with moving to an executive committee role, but refers to challenges faced when the interviewee took a big step up to a managerial position – a similarly big step up to the one the interviewees reported when they talked about moving to the executive committee. The interviewee is now a member of her organization's top management team:

> I went to a managerial level overnight. I had to convince senior people that marketing had a role to play. I had to convince them that they had to get involved in order to get the desired effects. I had to sell it into them and say 'trust me'. In the first few months, however, they found it difficult to trust me as I had not yet proved myself. I found that the only way around this was to explain the consequences of their inactions compared with the actions I needed them to take. When eventually the predicted outcome came about,

they realized I did know what I was talking about and I gained more credibility. If I had been a man, I don't think I would have needed to prove myself; they would have taken a man's advice on trust. (Monique Dumas, Investor Relations and Communications Partner, Electra Partners)

Clearly, establishing credibility and building trust remains a challenge throughout a woman's career and she has to work hard to overcome initial distrust.

LESSONS LEARNED

I know what I'm talking about

Soon after starting their new roles and working with their new colleagues on the executive committee, the interviewees realized they did know what they were talking about, and that despite the challenges they could do the job:

> Despite the challenges, it all felt very natural. As a woman you need to be confident that you are really, really good at something. And this role confirmed that I was really good at solving business problems and communicating them. When my confidence is shaken I go back to those basics – it's a natural reaction. I work out what my boss wants and communicate really well. Most women have enormous self-doubt. You need to have confidence at the senior level. You are surrounded by men, it is an aggressive environment. (Carolyn Fairbairn, Group Development and Strategy Director, ITV)

> It was not as scary to work at board level as I thought it would be. I thought 'Yes, I know what I am talking about.' (Senior manager, FTSE 100 company)

Building senior management relationships

Once they are members of executive committees, the women start interacting with the most senior people in the organization on a daily basis as their peers. This experience gives the interviewees the opportunity to further fine-tune their interpersonal skills. The interviewees talked about learning to influence across the organization and about using a very rational approach to influence the CEO and various other senior colleagues:

> I had to interact with a lot of new people at senior level outside the board to get the work done for the board. This helped me to learn how to influence in a large corporation. (Senior manager, FTSE 100 company)

> I learned to be less emotional. I had to be even-keeled and rational as I had to influence the finance director and the CEO. (Senior manager, FTSE 100 company)

Working under pressure

Working under pressure was not a new experience for the interviewees but it took on a new dimension as the deliverables became even more visible than before because the woman's new boss was the CEO of the organization. As we saw earlier, the move to the executive committee is often perceived as a big step up, with many new challenges. It takes time to master these and to become familiar with the new roles. Working long hours was often mentioned in connection with this critical job assignment. The following comments highlight the importance of emotional intelligence when it comes to dealing effectively with the pressures of a senior management role. Emotional intelligence was introduced when we looked at the first of the critical job assignments in this book – the early stretch assignment. By the time women get to the senior management level, they will have been able to develop their understanding of their own and others' feelings, but it is still a challenge they face and their skills have to be fine-tuned further:

> I enjoy crisis management. I learned in previous roles to manage multiple projects and not to blow up in the process. I can manage myself and my stress. It's about self-preservation. (Senior manager, FTSE 100 company)

> I learned to be cautious and not to overload people even though I have the energy myself to work toward demanding goals. (Senior manager, FTSE 100 company)

I have learned to admit to mistakes and am ready to change if my strategy doesn't work. I have an open door for people. It is all about emotional intelligence. (Senior manager, FTSE 100 company)

CAREER BENEFITS

A wider influencing and decision-making remit

As part of their role on the executive team, women start to run the organization jointly with their colleagues. A number of the interviewees talked about the need to be able to talk knowledgably about wider business issues and not just about their own functions. As part of their job they get involved in wider decision-making, which extends beyond their functional roles, and their sphere of influence increases significantly:

I have now moved beyond a pure functional role. As a member of the executive committee one is expected to provide broader comment and advice. I also chair the operational risk committee. Overall there is more breadth and I also have much more influence.'(Amanda MacKenzie, Group Marketing Director, Aviva)

I got involved in managerial decisions and not just M&A decisions. It was an opportunity for me to see the board work: minutes, decision-making, networking with very senior people. It also gave me international exposure. (Senior manager, FTSE 100 company)

Working directly for the CEO was great recognition for me and my role within the organization. It gave me greater opportunities to influence across the business. (Senior manager, FTSE 100 company)

I control these areas and now have the power to say 'I don't like how that looks.' (Senior manager, FTSE 100 company)

Delivering results at the most senior level

In addition to the challenges of being a member of the executive committee and reporting directly to the CEO, there are, of course, also the challenges of the role itself. The functional or general management responsibilities that these roles bring are significant:

> I ran a team of 70 and had a budget of over £100m. I achieved so much: I launched six new [products] and implemented five or six game-changing things for the organization. During this time I felt in control. (Senior manager, FTSE 100 company)

It is at this most senior level that the interviewees demonstrated they can be relied upon to deliver: 'Give me anything and it will be delivered on time.' The rules of the game have therefore not changed. Just as showing that they can and will deliver results has been a career accelerator for the interviewees during all the preceding phases of their careers, it still applies now. However, delivering results now takes place in an even more complex environment: 'I am good at what I do and respected for it. I deliver and always beat expectations. My CEO has seen me deal with complex projects and knows that I am confident in difficult situations' (Senior manager, FTSE 100 company).

To deliver these results, a number of the interviewees talked about the importance of drawing on previous experience:

> My goal was to apply all the lessons learned from before. Within two to three months I felt I had achieved a lot in this new role. I quickly got the right team and strategy in place and aligned the resources around what needed to be done. When I look back I feel I showed myself that I can apply the lessons I had learned. (Karen Oddey, CEO of an equity-funded specialist electronics company)

SUPPORT

A manager's support is still important for this critical job assignment, but this time around the boss is the CEO of a FTSE 100 company. The type of support the interviewees talked about receiving from their CEOs was quite diverse. Some of the women talked about being inspired by their CEOs, others talked about the praise and therefore the recognition they had been given by their CEOs, and yet others talked about the practical support they had received. One interviewee, for example, talked about how her CEO allowed her to work from home one day a week after she had her first child. He made this possible because he was keen to keep her in the team. This arrangement also allowed him to telephone her while she was working at home to talk about confidential business matters. Working directly for the CEO is demanding, and a few of the interviewees who talked about this critical job assignment reiterated the importance of having a good direct team, which allowed them to create some head room for themselves. The importance of gaining headroom was discussed in the context of people management in Chapter 7. The more senior women get, the more they have to delegate the day-to-day running of their parts of the organization to allow them to focus on strategy and to develop a vision for their area of work.

TIMING

By the nature of the role, this is a job assignment that will come later in a woman's career. In many cases, it is the pinnacle of a woman's career. Some of the interviewees, however, obtained executive committee positions in their FTSE 100 companies in their thirties. These are rare cases where women have moved to very senior and influential positions very quickly. The average age of the interviewees with executive board positions was 47. Of the 36 interviewees who are members of an executive committee, half also hold a non-executive director position, some of these being with FTSE 100 organizations. Two-thirds of the women at this level have children.

SUMMARY

Becoming a member of an executive committee means breaking through the glass ceiling. Making it to this level is a formidable task and the interviewees who succeeded had to overcome many hurdles and prove themselves to be reliable deliverers of outstanding results time and again. And it is this delivery that still very much counts at this level. Despite reaching the most senior level in an organization, many of the interviewees experienced a temporary dip in confidence and had to find their voice again in this very male arena. They soon realized, however, that they were well-equipped to deal with the challenges of their new roles. Building new relationships quickly at this senior level and integrating with the new team are vital. The support that is important for the interviewees now comes from their CEO, either in the form of practical support, inspiration or praise and recognition. This role is usually reserved for a later point in a woman's career; the average age of the interviewees who were members of an executive committee was 47. However, there were a few interviewees who joined the executive committee of their organizations in their thirties.

TAKING ACTION

- **Making your name.** How will you make your name to help you move to this most senior level in an organization? Highly visible and highly valued change management, turnaround or intrapreneurial assignments may help you to stand out. Decide what your most effective leadership brand is and start building it.
- **Building trust.** You need credibility, and the current members of the executive committee, and in particular the CEO, have to be convinced of your potential as a business leader. What are your opportunities to build relationships with people at this most senior level? You may also have to explore new avenues for networking, as your first role on an executive committee may be in an organization other than your current one. How can you widen your network?
- **Drawing on inner confidence.** Moving to an executive committee role requires confidence. Not only confidence once you get there but also the confidence that you are able to take this big step. Do not be held back by self-limiting beliefs, a lack of career planning and a lack of strategic networking. Now is the time to draw on your most senior sponsors and to think strategically about your next move. Executive committees are still the domain of men, and without stating clearly your desire to move to this level, your CEO may assume that you are not interested in taking on more responsibility.

PART III

13

CONCLUSION: WHERE TO NEXT?

The playing field for women is not level, and the cultural and structural hurdles they encounter make their ascent to senior positions in business more difficult. There is much that organizations, government and society at large can do to make it easier for women to advance: flexible working arrangements; extending the time horizons of the definition of high-potential; emphasizing and supporting the role of fathers; and senior management diversity education are just a few of the many elements that can make a difference. Many of these changes are cultural and require a change in attitudes. As we saw in Chapter 10, cultural change is difficult to achieve and it will take more time until the playing field is level, or at least more level, for women. In the meantime, there are things that women can do to help themselves to progress in their careers, as the career histories of the interviewees in this book have showed. I have summarized them here as the five Cs:

* Career planning;
* Critical job assignments;
* Courage;
* Curiosity; and
* Connectedness.

CAREER PLANNING

While we cannot foresee all the challenges we might encounter in our careers, Adair advises that if we look hard enough ahead and think about our passions and talents, we can see what kinds of challenges may lie ahead of us.[1] Thus we can prepare ourselves and be ready to face challenges as we come across them. Thinking more carefully about the different types of assignments that allow us both to develop personally and to gain professional credibility will help us to navigate around the additional hurdles of gender bias, stereotypes and the challenges of combining the demands of executive life with bringing up children.

The interviewees reported that, while they did not have concrete, long-term career plans, they were all curious, wanted to learn, and were ready to seize career opportunities as they emerged. They were also well-connected with former bosses and in many cases had senior sponsors. They also evaluated carefully the various opportunities on offer at any given time. They took concrete career decisions to broaden out or to seek specific experiences such as operational responsibility. Finally, when they encountered particularly difficult transition points, such as toward the end of their career, where commitment, outstanding results and sponsorship were no longer enough to progress, they began to engage in more planned career activities, including targeted networking and addressing the skills gaps on their CVs.

As women face more hurdles along the way, career planning is vital in order to avoid the many off-ramps or dead ends that often arise.

CRITICAL JOB ASSIGNMENTS

Critical job assignments build credible CVs and develop essential leadership qualities, and are therefore key to a woman's career progression. Without the right assignments and experiences, the much-needed senior management endorsement of 'Your record stands before you. You are tried and tested' will not be provided.

In the preceding chapters I have described nine critical job assignments that the 53 interviewees who took part in the study underpinning this book identified as being critical for both their personal development and their career progression (see Figure 13.1).

The majority of the senior women who made it to the top started off on the fast track with an early stretch assignment which brought with it some formidable challenges and often long hours, but it also rewarded the women with increased personal confidence, access to senior management and that all-important senior management sponsorship. Roles from there onwards tend to be diverse and increasingly gritty. Learning to manage people and getting the best out of them; working in different environments and taking on assignments abroad; and, very important, exposure to operational roles, are vital during the next phase. These roles establish a woman at middle management level and

IN FOCUS: THE CRITICAL JOB ASSIGNMENTS MODEL

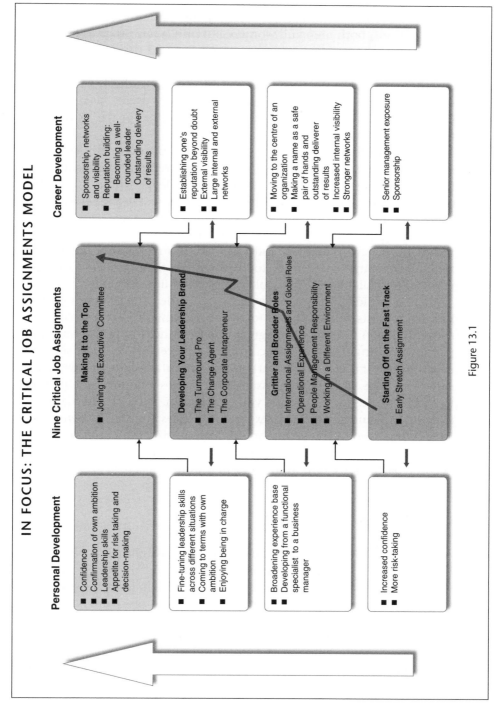

Figure 13.1

start to move her toward senior roles. There are many good people in organizations, both men and women, but only a few progress to senior roles. To get there, women have to stand out and develop their leadership brand. The roles that are particularly valued by organizations and therefore most effective for establishing one's leadership brand are those of change agent, turnaround pro or intrapreneur. Making-your-name assignments put women on the starting line for the next move to the executive committee.

As a woman goes through the nine different job assignments she gains (a) a reputation and (b) visibility for (c) being a well-rounded leader with (d) excellent organizational and business knowledge who is (e) capable of delivering outstanding results time and again. As a result, senior managers are much more likely to open doors to even greater opportunities for these women. Underpinning the continued delivery of results are the many personal qualities and insights the interviewees mentioned as the development skills they took away from their critical job assignments. We shall take a closer look at these later in the chapter.

There is no ideal timing or sequencing of the nine different critical job assignments. Becoming too focused on following a certain path will certainly mean missing many great opportunities along the way, and possibly missing the final goal completely. Nevertheless, there seem to be a number of roles that are particularly important early in a woman's career, such as early stretch assignments; roles that are much easier to tackle while not caring for young children, such as international assignments and operational experience. Roles that lend themselves to building a senior leadership brand, such as intrapreneurial ventures, large-scale change management projects and turnaround assignments become particularly important later in a woman's career.

COURAGE AND CURIOSITY

As women work through various critical job assignments they learn important developmental lessons. The first one is about courage, which I have defined in a broad sense here. It includes being prepared to take risks and make decisions even when the outcome is not 100 percent certain. It is also about taking on new challenges, a leap of faith and that deep breath in when a woman is thinking 'Can I really do this?' but then still goes ahead. Furthermore, it is about the courage 'to become visible' and to seek posts with visible outcomes, such as sales roles. It is also about being brave enough to assume additional authority as well as additional responsibilities. And last, but definitely not least, it is about the courage to ask – for a promotion, an international assignment or more responsibility. As one senior interviewee's comment at the start of Chapter 9 showed, we should ask ourselves continually 'What is the worst that can happen?'

The next lesson is about the importance of curiosity. By the term curiosity I mean showing an interest in new assignments, in working abroad, in giving a new process a go, and being open to learning from others. It is about acquiring a broad career basis by trying different roles, and, as we saw, the interviewees developed greatly by embracing different challenges. But it is also about a curious business mind that allows a woman to ask questions about the business and to enquire why things are done the way that they are. Looking left and right and seriously considering unusual opportunities such as secondments, committee work and charity work are also important. Let us refer back briefly to the observation of an HR director in Chapter 4, that none of the female management trainees were interested in taking on the opportunity to work with one of the most senior people in the organization on a daily basis, as they felt this did not fit with the career path they had mapped out for themselves. While this is only an anecdotal observation, it reflects what almost all the interviewees talked about: the importance of seizing opportunities when they present themselves, which requires both curiosity and courage.

CONNECTEDNESS

This is about learning that you cannot do it alone. Without the right connections and support network no woman is likely to succeed. The most important people for women are a supportive boss, a sponsor, a supportive partner and a high-performing team. Managers and sponsors take important roles in supporting women, opening doors, pointing to the importance of certain experiences and helping to boost confidence when it has ebbed momentarily. Supportive partners or significant others provide emotional support, regularly say 'You can do it', and where there are children, often help to share the additional childcare responsibilities.

Many of the assignments the interviewees talked about were obtained through personal contacts. As the interviewees became more senior and were proving themselves to be reliable deliverers, sponsors increasingly sought them out for ever more challenging assignments.

A REMINDER: SELF-DOUBTS AND SETBACKS

All the interviewees are very capable and impressive women who have succeeded in breaking through the glass ceiling and over-come many hurdles along the way; many of them while also hav-ing children. However, all of them are very human, too, and were extremely open about the self-doubt and setbacks they had suf-fered occasionally. The In Focus section in Chapter 11 discussed how a number of interviewees had taken time out or a step back to recharge batteries after burning out from juggling the challenges of an executive career combined with raising a young family. After a setback, some introspection took place; however, the interviewees were soon back on track, taking on new opportunities and putting themselves forward for new challenges. Let us remind ourselves of one of the comments at the start of Chapter 12:

> People who have made it to the top haven't had a smooth ride. They have messed up something. Women can take it very personally. Men are better at externalizing. Be more male and blame the environment – something was not right. It is impor-tant to bounce back and keep going. (Helen Buck, Convenience Director, J. Sainsbury)

Women need resilience to overcome the many hurdles on their way to the top.

CAREER INTELLIGENCE

The five Cs of career planning, critical job assignments, courage and curiosity, and connectedness make a woman career intelligent. I am borrowing Arthur and colleagues' term of the intelligent career, which we briefly encountered in Chapter 3.[2] The senior women who took part in the study underpinning this book are all undoubtedly cognitively intelligent, and many talked about the importance of developing and fine-tuning their emotional intelligence. Despite their admission that they did not have career plans, I would argue that all of them have been very career intelligent in that they have met many of the criteria of an intelligent career. They *know what* is important for their careers by picking important critical job assignments; they *know how* to be a credible leader by taking on board important development lessons through the critical job assignments; they *know why* they are taking certain actions and are clearly driven by courage and curiosity; they *know with whom* to network and they understand the importance of connectedness. Until the playing field has been levelled, being career intelligent is an important way in which women can help themselves to navigate the additional hurdles as effectively as possible.

APPENDIX: RESEARCH BACKGROUND

As part of the Women Leaders Study, a total of 53 interviews were conducted, 26 as face-to-face interviews and 27 as telephone interviews. Both senior women and senior men were interviewed for the purpose of this study, but biographical information was only collected from those women who talked about their personal career experiences and not from those interviewees who took part in the study to give views about women's career development in the role of subject matter expert.

Biographical information

The interviewees' average age was 45 years. The youngest interviewee was aged 28 and the oldest 63. The average number of years of work experience was 22 years. The sample included a small number of middle-management women. A number of the interviewees have retired from executive life and hold a portfolio of non-executive directorships. Information about other biographical indicators is given in Figures A1.1–A1.7 and Table A1.1 below.

As is to be expected, there were some demographic differences among the interviewees when split according to organizational levels.

The interviewees represented a wide range of different industry sectors and functions.

Critical job assignments

A total of 112 different critical job assignments were explored during the interviews. On average, two assignments per interviewee were recorded, but some interviewees discussed up to four different critical job assignments during their interview. The accounts of the different

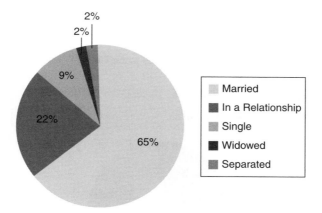

Figure A1.1 **Marital status of interviewees**

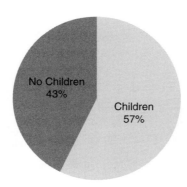

Figure A1.2 **Number of interviewees with children**

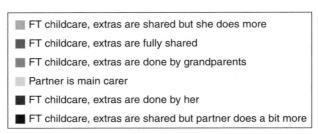

- FT childcare, extras are shared but she does more
- FT childcare, extras are fully shared
- FT childcare, extras are done by grandparents
- Partner is main carer
- FT childcare, extras are done by her
- FT childcare, extras are shared but partner does a bit more

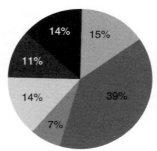

Figure A1.3 **Division of labor among interviewees' families regarding childcare**

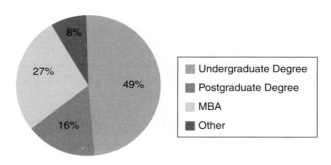

Figure A1.4 **Education level of interviewees**

TABLE A1.1 Organizational levels of interviewees

	Middle management	Senior management – just below board level	Member of executive board	Member of executive board, some non-executive directorships	Retired from executive position, portfolio of non-executive directorships	Total
Numbers	6	4	18	18	3	**49**
Average age	32	40	45	48	57	**45**
Average number of years in the workplace	9	16	23	26	34	**22**

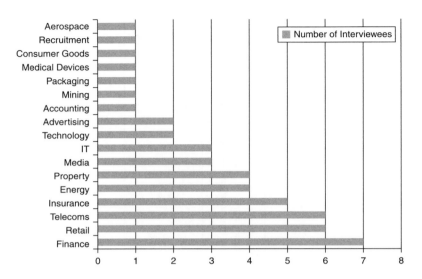

Figure A1.5 **Industry sectors represented by interviewees**

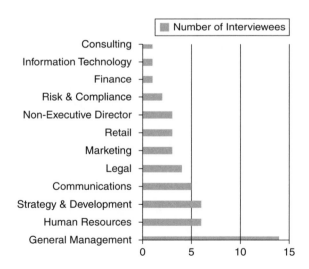

Figure A1.6 **Functions represented among interviewees**

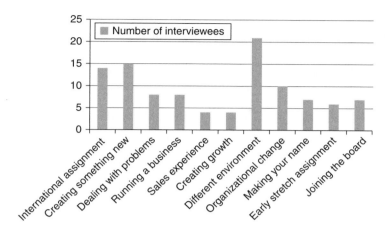

Figure A1.7 **Critical job assignments cited most frequently by interviewees**

assignments were categorized into fifteen different groups. The most frequently cited ones are listed in Figure A1.7.

Data analysis

The nature of the data analysis conducted for the Women Leader Study is qualitative, which means that the interview transcripts were evaluated for common themes and the analysis focuses on bigger picture trends. The numbers in this study are too small to be able to draw any firm statistical conclusions.

Not all of the experiences the interviewees talked about fell neatly into one of the nine critical job assignment categories. For example, a global role will bring all the challenges of working across continents and learning to deliver to different cultures, but it often also brings other significant challenges, such as setting up a new business. As such, this experience spans two different categories. Where this was the case, the experience was logged against the category into which it seemed to fit best. The data logged against each of the nine categories of critical job assignment was examined to establish its main job- and women-specific challenges, lessons learned, career benefits, support and timing. However, where a critical job assignment also contained elements of another assignment, the data were also examined in relation to the second assignment. The aim was to make the accounts of each of the job assignments as rich in information as possible. While this may be classed as double counting, the primarily qualitative nature of the analysis has not been affected adversely by this approach. Potential double counting of data becomes more of an issue with quantitative analysis, so where quantitative analysis methods were used, each critical job assignment was counted only once.

NOTES AND REFERENCES

INTRODUCTION

1. Timeline: 50 years of Catalyst. Available at www.catalyst.org.
2. Joint Council for Qualifications: GCSE, Applied GCSE and Entry Level Certificate Results, Summer 2010. Available at: www.jcq.org.uk.
3. Joint Council for Qualifications: A, AS and AEA Results, Summer 2010. Available at: www. jcq.org.uk.
4. Office for National Statistics, published 26 November 2007.
5. P. Cappelli and M. Hamori (2005). The new road to the top. *Harvard Business Review*, January.
6. Equalities and Human Rights Commission (2008). *Sex and Power. A Snail's Progress*. Manchester. UK: EHRC.
7. S. Vinnicombe, R. Sealy, J. Graham and E. Dolder (2010). The Female FTSE 100 Board Report 2010. Opening up the Appointment Process. Cranfield, UK: Cranfield School of Management.

CHAPTER 1

1. L. Joy, N. M. Carter, H. M. Wagner and S. Narayanan (2007). *The Bottom Line: Corporate Performance and Women's Representation on Boards*. New York: Catalyst.
2. G. Morse (2002). The emancipated organization. Insights on gender, leadership, and power formed over 25 years on the front lines: A conversation with Kim Campbell. *Harvard Business Review*, September.
3. M. A. Mason and E. Mason Ekman (2008). *Mothers on the Fast Track: How a New Generation Can Balance Family and Careers*. New York: Oxford University Press.
4. J. Evetts (2000). Analysing change in women's careers: culture, structure and action dimensions. *Gender, Work & Organization*, 7, 57–67.
5. See notes 3 and 4.
6. G. Desvaux, S. Devillard-Hoellinger and M. C. Meaney (2008). A business case for women. *McKinsey Quarterly*, September.
7. S. Wellington, M. Brumit Kropf and P. R. Gerkovich (2003). What's holding women back? *Harvard Business Review*, June.
8. D. E. Meyerson and J. K. Fletcher (2000). A modest manifesto for shattering the glass ceiling. *Harvard Business Review*, January.
9. A. H. Eagly and L. L. Carli (2007). Women and the labyrinth of leadership. *Harvard Business Review*, September.
10. See note 7.

11. R. Fecteau (2008). Teaching future CIOs the ropes. Available at: www.CIO.com.
12. See note 7.
13. Also often referred to as staff roles.
14. B. White, C. Cox and C. Cooper (1992). *Women's Career Development. A Study of High-Flyers*. Oxford: Basil Blackwell.
15. C. Cox and C. Cooper (1988). *High Flyers*. Oxford: Basil Blackwell.
16. See note 14.
17. M. W. McCall and M. M. Lombardo (1983). *Off the Track: Why and How Successful Executives Get Derailed*. Greensboro, NC: Center for Creative Leadership.
18. J. Adair (2005). *How to Grow Leaders: The Seven Key Principles of Effective Leadership Development*. London: Kogan Page.
19. M. W. McCall, M. M. Lombardo and A. M. Morrison (1988). *Lessons of Experience. How Successful Executives Develop on the Job*. New York: The Free Press.
20. W. P. Macaux (2009). Making the most of stretch assignments: a white paper. Available at: http://www.generativityllc.com/archives.htm.
21. See note 18.
22. See note 18.
23. D. L. Dotlich, J. L. Noel and N. Walker (2004). *Leadership Passages. The Personal and Professional Transitions That Make or Break a Leader*. San Francisco: Jossey-Bass.
24. See note 19.
25. See note 23.
26. C. D. McCauley (1999). *Learning from Work Experience. The Job Challenge Profile*. San Francisco: Jossey-Bass/Pfeiffer.
27. S. R. Madsen (2008). *On Becoming a Woman Leader. Learning from the Experiences of University Presidents*. San Francisco: Jossey-Bass.

CHAPTER 2

1. S. Mavin (2001). Women's career in theory and practice: time for change? *Women in Management Review*, 16, 183–92.
2. B. White (1995). The career development of successful women. *Women in Management Review*, 10, 4–15.
3. A. M. Morrison, R. P. White and E. Van Velsor (1987). *Breaking the Glass Ceiling*. Reading, MA: Addison Wesley, cited in S. Mavin, (2001) Women's career in theory and practice: time for change? *Women in Management Review*, 16, 183–92.
4. M. A. Mason and E. Mason Ekman (2007). *Mothers on the Fast Track. How a New Generation Can Balance Family and Careers*. Oxford: Oxford University Press.
5. A. Russell Hochschild, with A. Machung (2003). *The Second Shift*. New York: Penguin.
6. See note 4.
7. B. White, C. C. Cox and C. L. Cooper (1997). A portrait of successful women. *Women in Management Review*, 12, 27–34.
8. See note 2.
9. D. A. O'Neil and D. Bilimoria (2005). Women's career development phases: idealism, endurance and reinvention. *Career Development International*, 10, 168–89.
10. M. N. Ruderman and P. J. Ohlott (2002). *Standing at the Crossroads: Next Steps for High-Achieving Women*. San Francisco: Jossey-Bass.
11. See note 9.
12. See note 2.
13. See note 4.
14. See note 7.

15. P. Cappelli and M. Hamori (2005). The new road to the top. *Harvard Business Review*, January.
16. R. Simpson and Y. Altman (2000). The time bounded glass ceiling and young women managers: career progress and career success – evidence from the UK. *Journal of European Industrial Training*, 24, 190–8.
17. Forethought Data Point (Letters) (2007). Younger women at the top. *Harvard Business Review*, April.
18. G. Powell and D. Butterfield (1994). Investigating the glass ceiling phenomenon: an empirical study of actual promotions to top management. *Academy of Management Journal*, 37, 68–86.
19. See note 16.
20. See note 16.
21. D. T. Hall (1999). Accelerate executive development – at your peril! *Career Development International*, 4, 237–9.
22. C. Hempsall and R. Myatt. What are the psychological skills of effective leaders? Kaisen Consulting Ltd. Available at: www.kaisen.co.uk.
23. D. L. Dotlich and P. C. Cairo (2003). *Why CEOs Fail: The 11 Behaviours that Can Derail Your Climb to the Top – and How to Manage Them*. San Francisco: Jossey-Bass.
24. See note 9.
25. A. Ramaswami, G. F. Dreher, R. Bretz and C. Wiethoff (2010). Gender, mentoring, and career success: the importance of organizational context, *Personnel Psychology*, 63(2), 385–405.
26. See note 7.
27. See note 9.
28. See note 4.
29. J. Adair (2005). *How to Grow Leaders: The Seven Key Principles of Effective Leadership Development*. London: Kogan Page.
30. P. Baumgarten, G. Desvaux and S. Devillard (2007). What shapes careers: A. McKinsey global survey. *The McKinsey Quarterly*, November. Paris: McKinsey.
31. See note 4.
32. S. R. Ezzedeen and K. G. Ritchey (2009). Career advancement and family balance strategies of executive women. *Gender in Management. An International Journal*, Vol. 24, pp. 388–411.
33. See note 32.
34. See note 32.
35. National Center for Health Statistics, USA. Available at: www.cdc.gov/nchs.
36. Office of National Statistics, UK. Available at: www.statistics.gov.uk.
37. A. H. Eagly and L. L. Carli (2007). Women and the labyrinth of leadership. *Harvard Business Review*, September.
38. A. Borg and M. R. Clayman (2008). *Climbing the Technical Ladder: Obstacles and Solutions for Mid-Level Women in Technology*. Stanford, CA: Stanford University Press.
39. See note 7.
40. See note 4.
41. See note 32.
42. See note 7.
43. See note 32.
44. See note 9.
45. See note 9.
46. See note 7.
47. See note 9.
48. J. H. Greenhaus, G. A. Callanan, V. M. Godshalk (2010). *Career Management*. Thousand Oaks, CA: Sage.

49. M. Heffernan (2004). *The Naked Truth. A Working Woman's Manifesto on Business and What Really Matters*. San Francisco. Jossey-Bass.
50. C. Gallagher, with S. K. Golant (2000). *Going to the Top: A Road Map for Success from America's Leading Women Executives*. New York: Viking.
51. R. S. Kaplan (2008). Reaching your potential. *Harvard Business Review*, July.
52. See note 49.
53. M. B. Arthur, P. H. Claman, R. J. DeFillippi (1995). Intelligent enterprise, intelligent career. *Academy of Management Executive*, 9, 7–22.
54. C. Jones and R. J. DeFillippi (1996). Back to the future in film: combining industry and self-knowledge to meet career challenges of the 21st century. *Academy of Management Executive*, 10, 89–104.
55. See note 29.
56. See note 50.

CHAPTER 3

1. M. N. Ruderman, P. J. Ohlott and K. E. Kram (1996). *Managerial Promotion: The Dynamics for Men and Women*. Greensboro, NC: Center for Creative Leadership.
2. R. Charan, S. Drotter and J. Noel (2001). *The Leadership Pipeline: How to Build the Leadership-Powered Company*. San Francisco: Jossey-Bass.
3. See note 2.
4. See note 1.
5. Celine Lake poll as quoted in M. Conlin and W. Zellner (1999). The glass ceiling: the CEO still wears wingtips. Available at: www.Businessweek.com.
6. L. Sabattini (2008). *Unwritten Rules: What You Don't Know Can Hurt Your Career*. New York: Catalyst.
7. K. F. Kram and M. McCollom Hampton (2003). When women lead: the visibility–vulnerability spiral. In R. J. Ely, E. G. Foldy and M. A. Scully (eds), *Reader in Gender, Work and Organization*. Oxford: Wiley-Blackwell.
8. See note 1.
9. K. L. Proudford (2007). Isn't She Delightful? Creating relationships that get women to the top (and keep them there). In B. Kellerman and D. L. Rhode (eds), *Women and Leadership: The State of Play and Strategies for Change*. San Francisco: Jossey-Bass.
10. H. Ibarra (1993). Personal networks of women and minorities in management: a conceptual framework. *Academy of Management Review*, 18, 56–87.
11. M. J. Davidson and C. L. Cooper (1992). *Shattering the Glass Ceiling: The Woman Manager*. London: Paul Chapman.
12. L. Torres and M. L. Huffman (2004). Who benefits? Gender differences in returns to social network diversity. In N. DiTomaso and C. Post (eds), *Diversity in the Work Force*, Research in the Sociology of Work, Vol. 14. Bingley, UK: Emerald.
13. See note 6.
14. See note 6.
15. See note 1.
16. R.Simpson and Y. Altman (2000). The time bounded glass ceiling and young women managers: career progress and career success – evidence from the UK. *Journal of European Industrial Training*, 24, 190–8.
17. C. Gallagher with S. K. Golant (2000). *Going to the Top: A Road Map for Success from America's Leading Women Executives*. New York: Viking.
18. M. Hennig and A. Jardim (1978). *The Managerial Woman*. London: Marion Boyars. As cited in B. White, C. Cox and C. Cooper (1992). *Women's Career Development. A Study of High-Fliers*. Oxford: Basil Blackwell.

19. L. V. Still (1994). Where to from here? Women in management: the cultural dilemma. *Women in Management Review*, 9(4), 3–10.
20. G. Desvaux, S. Devillard-Hoellinger, and M. C. Meaney (2008). A Business case for women. *McKinsey Quarterly*, September.
21. McCracken, D. M. (2000). Winning the talent war for women: sometimes it takes a revolution. *Harvard Business Review*, November.
22. Meaney, M. C. (2008). Seeing beyond the woman: an interview with a pioneering academic and board member. *McKinsey Quarterly*, September.
23. L. Babcock, S. Laschever, M. Gelfand and D. Small (2003). Nice girls don't ask. Women negotiate less than men – and everyone pays the price. *Harvard Business Review*, October.
24. S. Maxfield, M. Shapiro, V. Gupta and S. Hass (2010). Gender and Risk: Women, Risk Taking and Risk Aversion. *Gender in Management. An International Journal*, 25, 586–604.
25. See note 24.
26. J. E. V. Johnson and P. I. Powell (1994). Decision making, risk and gender: are managers different? *British Journal of Management*, 5, 123–38.
27. C. Gallagher, with S. K. Golant (2000). *Going to the Top. A Road Map for Success from America's Leading Women Executives*. New York: Viking.
28. M. N. Ruderman and P. J. Ohlott (2002). *Standing at the Crossroads. Next Steps for High-Achieving Women*. San Francisco: Jossey-Bass.
29. N. J. Adler (2005). Leading beyond boundaries: the courage to enrich the world. In L. Coughlin, E. Wingard and K. Hollihan (eds), *Enlightened Power: How Women Are Transforming the Practice of Leadership*. San Francisco: Jossey-Bass.
30. P. Klaus (2005). Good girls don't brag, do they? In L. Coughlin, E. Wingard and K. Hollihan (eds), *Enlightened Power: How Women Are Transforming the Practice of Leadership*. San Francisco: Jossey-Bass.
31. G. W. Dudley and S. L. Goodson (2007). *The Psychology of Sales Call Reluctance. Earning What You're Worth*. Dallas, TX: Behavioural Science Research Press.
32. Wendy Kinney, cited in To get to the top speak up: get out here, exude power and purpose. Available at: www.advancingwomen.com.
33. S. Mavin (2001). Women's career in theory and practice: time for change? *Women in Management Review*, 16, 183–92.
34. G. J. Wood and M. Lindorff (2001). Sex differences in explanations for career progress. *Women in Management Review*, 16, 152–62.

CHAPTER 4

1. C. Cox and C. Cooper (1988). *High Flyers*. Oxford: Basil Blackwell.
2. B. White, C. Cox and C. Cooper (1992). *Women's Career Development. A Study of High-Flyers*. Oxford: Basil Blackwell.
3. D. L. Dotlich, J. L. Noel and N. Walker (2004). *Leadership Passages: The Personal and Professional Transitions That Make or Break a Leader*. San Francisco: Jossey-Bass.
4. D. Goleman (2004). *Working with Emotional Intelligence*. London: Bloomsbury.
5. C. Hempsall and R. Myatt (n.d.). What are the psychological skills of effective leaders? Kaisen Consulting Ltd. Available at: www.kaisen.co.uk.
6. D. L. Dotlich and P. C. Cairo (2003). *Why CEOs Fail. The 11 Behaviours That Can Derail Your Climb to the Top – and How to Manage Them*. San Francisco: Jossey-Bass.
7. W. P. Macaux (2009). Making the most of stretch assignments: a white paper. Available at: http://www.generativityllc.com/archives.htm.

8. S. C. DeRue and N. Wellman (2009). Developing leaders via experience. The role of developmental challenge, learning orientation, and feedback availability. *Journal of Applied Psychology*, 99, 859–75.

CHAPTER 5

1. M. S. Wilson and M. A. Dalton (1998). *International Success: Selecting, Developing and Supporting Expatriate Managers*. Greenboro, NC: Center for Creative Leadership.
2. Organization Resources Counselors Worldwide (2007). *2006 Worldwide Survey of International Assignment Policies and Practices*. New York: Organization Resources Counselors Worldwide, cited in S. Shortland (2009). Gender diversity in expatriation: evaluating theoretical perspectives. *Gender in Management: An International Journal*, 24(5), 365–86.
3. Organization Resources Counselors Worldwide (2008). *Dual Careers and International Assignments Survey*. New York: Organization Resources Counselors Worldwide. cited in S. Shortland (2009). Gender diversity in expatriation: evaluating theoretical perspectives. *Gender in Management: An International Journal*, 24(5), 365–86.
4. N. Forster (1999). Another 'glass ceiling'? The experiences of women professionals and managers on international assignments. *Gender, Work & Organization*, 6(2), 79–90.
5. M. Linehan and J. S. Walsh (2000). Work-family conflict and the senior female international manager. *British Journal of Management*, 11, 49–58.
6. See note 4.
7. See note 1.
8. J. P. Guthrie, R. A. Ash and C. D. Stevens (2003). Are women 'better' than men? Personality differences and expatriate selection. *Journal of Managerial Psychology*, 18(3), 229–43.
9. See note 5.
10. M. L. Connerley, R. L. Mecham and J. P. Strauss (2008). Gender differences in leadership competencies, expatriate readiness, and performance. *Gender in Management: An International Journal*, 23(5), 300–16.
11. M. Linehan and H. Scullion (2001). Challenges for female international managers: evidence from Europe. *Journal of Managerial Psychology*, 16, 215–28.
12. See note 11.
13. B. L. Kirkman, B. Rosen, C. B. Gibson, P. E. Tesluk and S. O. McPherson (2002). Five challenges to virtual team success: lessons from Sabre, Inc. *Academy of Management Executive*, 16(3), 67–79.
14. See note 1.
15. See note 4.
16. M. Dickmann and N. Doherty (2008). Exploring the career capital impact of international assignments within distinct organizational contexts. *British Journal of Management*, 19, 145–61.
17. J. A. Volkmar and K. L. Westbrook (2005). Does a decade make a difference? A second look at western women working in Japan. *Women in Management Review*, 20(7), 464–77.
18. R. Tzeng (2006). Gender issues and family concerns for women with international careers: female expatriates in Western multinational corporations in Taiwan. *Women in Management Review*, 21, 376–92.
19. See note 5.
20. N. M. Dixon (1994). *The Organizational Learning Cycle: How We Learn Collectively*. New York: McGraw-Hill, cited in M. S. Wilson and M. A. Dalton (1998). *International Success. Selecting, Developing and Supporting Expatriate Managers*. Greenboro, NC: Center for Creative Leadership.

21. See note 1.
22. See note 1.
23. M. Moore (2002). Same ticket, different trip: supporting dual-career couples on global assignments. *Women in Management Review*, 17, 61–7.
24. N. Adler (1994). Competitive Frontiers: Women Managing Across Boarders. *Journal of Management Development*, 13, 24–41.
25. See note 4.
26. See note 1.
27. See note 4.
28. See note 4.
29. See note 1.
30. H. Harris (2004). Global careers: work-life issues and the adjustment of women international managers. *Journal of Management Development*, 23, 818–32.
31. See note 18.
32. See note 1.

CHAPTER 6

1. R. Fecteau (2008). Teaching future CIOs the ropes. Available at: www.CIO.com.
2. S. Wellington, M. Brumit Kropf and P. R. Gerkovich (2003). What's holding women back? *Harvard Business Review*, June.
3. R. Charan, S. Drotter and J. Noel (2001). *The Leadership Pipeline. How to Build the Leadership-Powered Company*. San Francisco: Jossey-Bass.

CHAPTER 7

1. R. Charan, S. Drotter and J. Noel (2001). *The Leadership Pipeline: How to Build The Leadership-Powered Company*. San Francisco: Jossey-Bass.
2. R. Ashkenas (2010). How to build an A-team from day one. *Harvard Business Review*, May.
3. M. Dewhurst, M. Guthridge and E. Mohr (2009). Motivating people: getting beyond money. *McKinsey Quarterly*, November.
4. B. McMahon (2005). Crossing over: leadership that makes others want to follow. In L. Coughlin, E. Wingard and K. Hollihan (eds), *Enlightened Power: How Women Are Transforming the Practice of Leadership*. San Francisco: Jossey-Bass.
5. L. A. Hill (2007). Becoming the boss. *Harvard Business Review*, January.
6. M. N. Ruderman and P. J. Ohlott (2002). *Standing at the Crossroads: Next Steps for High-Achieving Women*. San Francisco: Jossey-Bass.
7. G. Evans (2005). Are we looking after each other? women leaders winning the game. In L. Coughlin, E. Wingard and K. Hollihan (eds), *Enlightened Power: How Women Are Transforming the Practice of Leadership*. San Francisco: Jossey-Bass.
8. D. DeVries and R. Kaiser (2003). Going Sour in the C Suite: What you Can Do About Executive Derailment. Presented at Maximising Executive Effectiveness – Developing Your Senior Leadership: A workshop hosted by the Human Resources Planning Society, Miami, November 1–18.
9. L. L. Carli and A. H. Eagly (2007). Overcoming Resistance to Women Leaders. The Importance of Leadership Style. In B. Kellerman and D. L. Rhode (eds), *Women and Leadership: The State of Play and Strategies for Change*. San Francisco: Jossey-Bass.
10. G. Desvaux and S. Devillard (2008). *Women Matter 2: Female Leadership, A Competitive Edge for the Future*. Paris: McKinsey and Company.

11. See note 9.
12. Institute of Leadership and Management and Management Today (2009). *Index of Leadership Trust 2009*. London: Institute of Leadership and Management.
13. See note 5.

CHAPTER 8

1. R. Charan, S. Drotter and J. Noel (2001). *The Leadership Pipeline. How to Build the Leadership-Powered Company*. San Francisco: Jossey-Bass.
2. M. W. McCall, M. M. Lombardo and A. M. Morrison (1988). *Lessons of Experience. How Successful Executives Develop on the Job*. New York: The Free Press.
3. D. L. Dotlich, J. L. Noel and N. Walker (2004). *Leadership Passages. The Personal and Professional Transitions That Make or Break a Leader*. San Francisco: Jossey-Bass.
4. M. N. Ruderman and P. J. Ohlott (2002). *Standing at the Crossroads. Next Steps for High-Achieving Women*. San Francisco: Jossey-Bass.
5. See note 2.

CHAPTER 9

1. G. Pinchot (1985). *Intrapreneuring: why you don't have to leave your organisation to become an entrepreneur*. New York: Harper & Row.
2. N. E. Thornberry (2003). Corporate entrepreneurship: teaching managers to be entrepreneurs. *Journal of Management Development*, 4, 329–44.
3. See note 2.
4. See note 2.
5. M. C. Mattis (2004). Women entrepreneurs: out from under the glass ceiling. *Women in Management Review*, 19(3), 154–63.
6. See note 1.
7. See note 1.
8. See note 1.
9. See note 1.
10. B. Antoncic, M. S. Cardon and R. D. Hisrich (2004). Internationalizing corporate entrepreneurship: the impact on global HR management, *Advances in Entrepreneurship, Firm Emergence and Growth*, 7, 173–97.
11. L. Hillstrom (n.d.) Intrapreneurship. Available at: www.referenceforbusiness.com; accessed 21 January 2011.
12. See note 1.
13. See note 1.
14. See note 1.
15. See note 1.
16. Personal conversation, January 2010, London. Available at: www.boardsforum.com.
17. G. Pinchot and R. Pellman (1999). *Intrapreneuring in Action: A Handbook for Business Innovation*. San Francisco: Berrett-Koehler.
18. C. Cox and R. Jennings (1995). The foundation of success: the development and characteristics of British entrepreneurs and intrapreneurs. *Leadership and Organizational Development Journal*, 16, 4–9.

CHAPTER 10

1. J. P. Kotter (2001). What leaders really do. *Harvard Business Review*, December.
2. E. Lawson and C. Price (2003). The psychology of change management. *McKinsey Quarterly*, June.
3. McKinsey Global Survey (2010). What successful transitions share: McKinsey global survey results. *McKinsey Quarterly*, March.
4. B. Senior (2002). *Organisational Change*. Harlow, UK: Pearson Education.
5. R. J. Lee and S. N. King (2001). *Discovering the leader in you: a guide to realising your personal leadership potential*. San Francisco: Jossey-Bass. Cited in M. N. Ruderman and P. J. Ohlott (2002). *Standing at the Crossroads: Next Steps for High-Achieving Women*. Greensboro, NC: Center for Creative Leadership.
6. C. Aiken and S. Keller (2009). The irrational side of change management. *McKinsey Quarterly*, April.
7. See note 3.
8. McKinsey Quarterly Interview (2010). Making the emotional case for change: an interview with Chip Health. *McKinsey Quarterly*, March.
9. See note 6.
10. See note 4.

CHAPTER 11

1. S. Slatter, D. Lovett and L. Barlow (2006). *Leading Corporate Turnaround: How Leaders Fix Troubled Companies*. Chichester, UK: John Wiley.
2. G. Desvaux, S. Devillard and S. Sancier-Sultan (2010). Women matter 3: women leaders, a competitive edge in and after the crisis. McKinsey and Company. Available at http://www.mckinsey.com/locations/swiss/news_publications/pdf/Women_Matter_3_English.pdf.
3. M. K. Ryan, S. A. Haslam and T. Postmes (2007). Reactions to the glass cliff: gender differences in the explanations for the precariousness of women's leadership positions. *Journal of Organizational Change Management*, 20, 182–97.
4. D. Brady, K. Isaacs, M. Reeves, R. Burroway and M. Reynolds (2011). Sector, size, stability and scandal: explaining the presence of female executives in Fortune 500 firms. *Gender in Management: An International Journal*, 26, 84 –104
5. See note 1.
6. McKinsey Quarterly Interview (2010). Making the emotional case for change: an interview with Chip Heath. *McKinsey Quarterly*, March.
7. See note 1.
8. J. Isern, M. C. Meaney and S. Wilson (2009). Corporate transformation under pressure. *McKinsey Quarterly*, April 9.
9. S. Slatter and D. Lovett (1999). *Corporate Turnaround: Managing Companies in Distress*. London: Penguin.
10. See note 1.

CHAPTER 12

1. Also sometimes referred to as operating board, senior management team or leadership team.

2. Grant Thornton International Business Report (2011). Available at: www. grantthorntonibos.com/Press-room/2011/women_in-senior_management.asp.
3. E. Holst and A. Busch (2010). *Führungskräfte-Monitor 2010*. Berlin: Deutsches Institut für Wirtschaftsforschung.
4. Catalyst (2010). *Statistical Overview of Women in the Workplace: United States*. New York: Catalyst.
5. G. Desvaux, S. Devillard-Hoellinger and P. Baumgarten (2007). *Women Matter: Gender Diversity, a Corporate Performance Driver*. Paris: McKinsey and Company.
6. G. Desvaux and S. Devillard (2008). *Women Matter 2. Female Leadership, a Competitive Edge*. Paris: McKinsey and Company.
7. G. Stahl and N. Mühling (2010). *Deutschlands Chefinnen. Wie Frauen es an die Unternehmensspitze schaffen*. Frankfurt/Hamburg/Munich: Odgers Berndtson.

CHAPTER 13

1. J. Adair (2005). How to Grow Leaders: The Seven Key Principles of Effective Leadership Development. London: Kogan Page.
2. M. B. Arthur, P. H. Claman and R. J. DeFillippi (1995). Intelligent enterprise, intelligent career. *Academy of Management Executive*, 9, 7–22.

INDEX